What Parents, Professionals and Aspies Themselves Are Saying about *Beyond the Wall* ...

"In *Beyond the Wall* Stephen Shore provides an unusually interesting, well-written and insightful autobiographical account of the life of a person with high-functioning autism/Asperger Syndrome. This is a "user-friendly" book: Stephen is a courteous and well-informed tour guide, who makes our visit with him both enjoyable and informative. Highly recommended."

— Bernard Rimland, Ph.D., director, Autism Research Institute

"Stephen's words softened my heart. They made me proud to be a fellow aspie. I am certain everyone who reads Stephen's book will come away inspired by his life's story, honored by his decision to share so much of who he is, and touched by his honesty and courage. More importantly, I am quite certain his readers will forever more look upon people with any difference, particularly those on the light end of autism or Asperger Syndrome, as fine and nobly interesting people who have so very much to offer this society we all share."

— Liane Holliday Willey, Ed.D., author of *Pretending to Be Normal: Living with Asperger Syndrome* and *Asperger Syndrome in the Family: Redefining Normal*

"Stephen Shore's unique perspective makes this autobiography a wonderful, inspirational and educational book. The author provides valuable practical information that will benefit both parents and professionals."

— Stanley D. Klein, Ph.D., co-editor, *You Will Dream New Dreams, Inspiring Personal Stories by Parents of Children with Disabilities*

"With the innocence of a child and the insight of a mature social scientist, not to mention a great deal of courage, Stephen Shore has written a compelling and touching account of autism and Asperger Syndrome. The combination of pure story telling and thoughtful insight makes this book a major contribution to our understanding of and appreciation for the experience of these disorders. Even more, in providing us glimpses into an extraordinary life, *Beyond the Wall* humbles us and urges us to once again rethink the power of the human brain and the human spirit."

   – Thomas J. Cottle, professor of education, Boston University

"Stephen's ability to articulate how it feels to be diagnosed on the autism spectrum is a perspective no parent or professional should be without. His humorous way of translating the autistic mind so as to debunk the disability and truly understand what's *Behind the Wall* is nothing short of remarkable. Both professionally and personally Stephen's contribution to the autism community is a gift to all who know him."

   – Alex Michaels, executive director, Educational Consultants
      of New England, Inc., and an adult with Asperger Syndrome

"Stephen's intellectual curiosity embraces his own personal history, and like a reconnaissance team after a bomb explodes (the autism bomb) he works to reconstruct, restore and accommodate in the hopes of mitigating the personal effects of this devastating syndrome on families and self. This book is a must read for all persons teaching and loving children and adults diagnosed with autism or Asperger Syndrome."

   – Eileen Berger, director, Office for Students with Disabilities,
      Salem State College

"Stephen Shore is a bright light in a very dark place. He held my hand through cyberspace and helped me to understand how my grandson might feel. By communicating with Stephen, I realized how much hope there is for our children and adults with autism …"

   – Nancy Herndon Cale, VP, Unlocking Autism, and
      grandmother of child with autism

Beyond the Wall

*Personal Experiences
with Autism and
Asperger Syndrome*

Beyond the Wall

*Personal Experiences
with Autism and
Asperger Syndrome*

SECOND EDITION

Stephen M. Shore

P.O. Box 23173
Shawnee Mission, Kansas 66283-0173
www.aapcpublishing.net

©2003 by Autism Asperger Publishing Co.
Second Edition 2003; Second printing 2004
P.O. Box 23173
Shawnee Mission, Kansas 66283-0173
www.aapcpublishing.net

Publisher's Cataloging-in-Publication
(provided by Quality Books, Inc.)

Shore, Stephen, 1961-
   Beyond the wall : personal experiences with Autism and Asperger syndrome / Stephen Shore. – 2nd ed.
   p. cm.
   Includes bibliographic references.
   Library of Congress Control Number: 2002115674
   ISBN: 1-931282-19-6

   1. Shore, Stephen, 1961- 2. Asperger's syndrome–Patients–Biography. 3. Autism–Patients–Biography.
   I. Title.

RC553.A88S56 2002   616.89'82'0092
                      QBI02-200895

This book is designed in Minion and Helvetica Neueland

Managing Editor: Kirsten McBride
Cover Design: Akihiro Takamatsu and Jose Estevez
Production Assistant: Ginny Biddulph
Interior Design/Production: Tappan Design

Printed in the United States of America

Table of Contents

Foreword

Stephen presents an optimistic view of Asperger Syndrome and high-functioning autism. It is refreshing to have his positive and constructive outlook. As a person with high-functioning autism myself, I can relate to many of Stephen's experiences, both as a young child and as an adult. One of the most valuable insights this book offers is helping individuals on the autism spectrum to understand the subtle intricacies of social interaction. It is like a roadmap for navigating the social world.

When I was in high school, I was constantly teased and bullied. I had absolutely no idea why the other kids chose me to tease. I was unable to figure out what I was doing wrong. Stephen's book provides practical advice on combating teasing. As I read through the book, I thought back to my own experiences. I went through almost 30 years of not knowing that people had subtle social cues that they sent to each other with eye movement and body posture. I did not know that people communicated with eye movements until I read about them in a book when I was almost 50 years old. Stephen's experiences will help many people have a more fulfilling life.

Friendships are often gained through shared interests. My best friends have similar interests in subjects I am interested in such as animal behavior or designing livestock equipment. Both Stephen and I strongly recommend the cultivation of interests.

Stephen also provides lots of practical information about employment. For example, he describes how he lost a good music teaching job because he failed to recognize faculty politics. People on the spectrum are usually good at jobs where they can utilize their special skills such as architectural drawing or computer programming. However, they often get into trouble with the social aspects of the job. I have heard several sad stories of talented persons losing their jobs when promoted into a management position that they could not handle. Stephen has an excellent section in the book to help employers understand the social limitations of a person on the spectrum. This will help employers to understand why their otherwise brilliant computer programmer, for example, has social difficulties. I really liked the suggestions for how to handle problems with misinterpreting the behavior of a person on the spectrum. One of Stephen's suggestions rang a bell with me. A boss should be asked to: "Let me know if I have offended someone so that misunderstandings do not develop and grow." In my own case, I did not realize that in some situations I appeared rude or abrupt. Stephen suggests that a boss should let the person on the spectrum know if he or she has unintentionally been hurtful or abrupt.

In my book *Thinking in Pictures*, I discussed how to get a job by selling my talents and showing a portfolio of my work. Stephen's book provides information that will help people keep their jobs by avoiding social mistakes. Stephen's book would have been very valuable to me when I was starting and developing my career.

– Temple Grandin
Author, *Thinking in Pictures*

Preface

Wher unique challenges face the person on the autism
spectrum? What is meant by the "autism spectrum" any
way? How does one relate to persons with autism and
Asperger Syndrome? Are they really that different from all the rest
of the people in the world? What causes autism spectrum disorder?

In this book I hope to explore these and other questions. I use
the word "explore" because there is so much more to learn about
autism and related disorders. Researchers and people who work in
the field of autism are increasingly coming up with data that will
one day resolve some of these questions. Until that happens, however, we all will continue to explore the uncharted territory of the
autism spectrum.

In addition to being an autobiography, this book represents my
search for knowledge about Asperger Syndrome and autism, how
it affects me, and how I might use this knowledge to help others on
the autism spectrum. There are three narrating voices in the book.
The first is the autobiographical voice that tells the story of my life.
The second is what I call the time shifter. This voice describes
events in my life that are relevant to the topic at hand but are out
of sync with the strict chronological order of an autobiography.
The third is the researcher voice. In my quest for more knowledge
about myself as I relate to Asperger Syndrome and autism, I have
examined some of the literature to see how it relates to me and the
work I do with children on the autism spectrum. As a result of the
three-voice method, some of the chapters are very conversational
and autobiographical whereas others, particularly towards the end
of the book, get rather theoretical. This is how I make sense of my
life. Hopefully this presentation will make sense to the reader too.

Starting with Chapter One, I take a snapshot of what my life looks like today ... as an adult with the residuals of the autism spectrum disorder. Chapter Two goes back in time, starting from my birth where I seemed to develop at a slightly faster-than-normal rate until the autism bomb hit. Where did this bomb come from and what caused it? Some people point to genetic and environmental influences, vaccinations and other causes. Some have even attributed my situation to an emotional cause. While I am tempted to say that we do not have a clue, I think the prognosis for finding the etiology of autism is better than that. The problem is that there are too many scattered clues that need better organization and more direct correlation to autism. Perhaps in time we will find out that what we now consider the autism spectrum is a series of separate disorders causes that present themselves in a very similar manner.

Chapter Three depicts the period when I sink into autism. While I have some memories, I have relied heavily on my parents for descriptions of what they did with me and how I behaved and functioned in those years. At that time there was no concept of early intervention. Ignoring the professionals' call for separating me from my home and the environment I knew, my parents did what they thought was "right." Chapter Four, the Putnam Period, looks at my experience in a special school for children with "atypical development." For this material, I am indebted to my nursery school teacher. In this edition, Chapter Five on my nursery school years contains an expanded portion devoted to how sensory issues may affect people with Asperger Syndrome and autism. Chapters Six, Seven, and Eight cover my years in public school. They started out as a social and educational disaster. But contrary to the experiences of many people with autism or other differences, things got better in middle and high school as I learned how to better relate to the environment and discovered the joys of producing music with others.

College and work experiences comprise Chapters Nine, Ten, and Eleven. While college was, and continues to be, a sort of paradise for me, the world of work and what some consider as reality was not. With an emphasis placed on learning and creativity, educational institutions seem to be much more forgiving of individual differences than the business universe of accounting and finance that I encountered. As a result, my work remains and I expect will continue to be concentrated in the world of academia. With more people on the autism spectrum now seeking higher education, I have included new material on choosing a college that best matches the student (see Appendix B). In addition, a section has been added on steps to prepare a person for the challenges of self-advocacy as he or she transitions to postsecondary education as well as the workplace and community.

In the remaining chapters, the writing of this autobiography and my life begin to intersect. This is where the sleeping dragon of autism reawakened and drove me on a quest to find out more about this way of being and its relation to me. I use this term "way of being" rather than "disorder" because I wonder whether the autism spectrum should be considered as "another order" of being as opposed to a disordered, deviant way of existing. Societal constructs relating to how others compare those with autism and Asperger Syndrome to the rest of society play a heavy role in this respect. Revisiting autism by relating to and working with others who have autism and examining how to best disclose one's placement on the autism spectrum to others has helped me hone in on and analyze what autism means to me.

This book represents my search for answers to the many questions I have about autism and Asperger Syndrome and how I can use my personal experiences and research to help make lives easier for others on the autism spectrum.

Stephen M. Shore
Brookline, Massachusetts

Acknowledgments

This book was made possible with the assistance and encouragement from many people who believed in me. My parents' refusal to place me in an institution, despite initial recommendations from professional evaluators, and the continued unconditional love, acceptance and support from my Mom and Dad, siblings, Robin and Martin, all of my grandparents, and later my wife, Yi Liu, have been a never-ending source of strength to me.

Many thanks to individuals such as Susan Zurawski, who introduced me to the Language and Cognitive Development Center (LCDC) in Jamaica Plain, Massachusetts, as we awaited the beginning of a lecture by Dr. Temple Grandin. I am grateful to many others at LCDC such as Dr. Paul Callahan, Kristina Chretien, Lucy Hooper, Suzanne Martel and, of course, the children of the school, who have given me invaluable insights into both myself and how to work with individuals with autism.

Special thanks are also in order to the director of the Language and Cognitive Development Center, Dr. Arnold Miller, who opened his school and his heart in order to create a place of learning and discovery for all of those involved. Without his continual assistance and support as primary reviewer and editor of this manuscript before it was accepted for publication, this book would never have gotten off the ground, nor continued to its completion.

Dear friends such as Phyllis (the art professor) Akillian, Michael J. Biundo, Ph. D., Jean-Paul Bovee, Sandy D'Erasmo, Andrea DeSante, Neal Goodman, Dania Jekel, MSW, Stanley Klein, Ph. D., Sarah and Steven Knudsen, Ann Larkin, Ph. D., Karen Levine, Ed. D., Stephanie Loo, Sharon Lowenstien, Ed. D., Alex Michaels, Jerry Newport, Pamela Oliver, Karen and Sam Pandolfi, Barbara Pichler, my nursery school teacher, Nancy Reiser, Dr. Daniel Rosenn, Louise

Ross, Ed. D., Cathy, Jerry and Zachariah Silbert, Philip Schwarz, Laurie Smith, and Eileen Torchio, have all offered invaluable feedback as they read through all or parts of *Beyond the Wall* as a work in progress and/or provided invaluable help as I wrote the second edition. Many other people touched my life during this journey. To those whom I have inadvertently left out of this acknowledgment, only to remember them after the book goes to print, please accept my apologies along with my heartfelt thanks as your contributions were also vital to making this book as it is today.

Many thanks are in order to the Higashi School of Boston for Autism for providing the artwork for the cover. In response to my inquiry about possibly obtaining artwork, the executive director, Robert Fantasia, led me to two wonderful people, Akihiro Takamatsu (Mr. T.) and Jose Estevez. Mr. Takamatsu, who loves all kinds of art, began working at Boston Higashi as a classroom teacher of young students and is now in his 14th year teaching there. Prior to that he taught in Higashi School in Tokyo for three and a half years. Mr. Takamatsu is one of the few remaining original members of the Higashi School staff from Japan who has brought Daily Life Therapy to the United States as developed by Dr. Kiyo Kitahara in Tokyo.

The picture on the cover was drawn by Jose Estevez, a young man with autism who has been at Higashi for almost eight years. The drawing of the tree, located outside of his classroom window, was completed in about an hour and a half, over a series of morning sessions while Jose waited for his school day to begin. He still draws every day and uses this medium of expression to appreciate the seasonal changes of nature as reflected by this tree. Akihiro Takamatsu and I spent a cold, blustery day taking pictures of me in various areas of the school, and then Mr. Takamatsu artfully placed them in collage fashion on top of Jose's drawing.

Finally, I wish to express my appreciation for the wonderful editing and support from my editor, Kirsten McBride. Her help in making this long, winding, almost 300-page manuscript, in addition to the 2nd edition, presentable to you, the reader, was immeasurable in making *Beyond the Wall* what it is today.

The Castle

Imagine that you are trying to reach a young prince locked inside a huge castle. First, you must cross the wide moat, which is filled with hungry alligators. Once across, you must find a way into the castle. Arriving inside you see armed guards everywhere.

You must find your way past the guards as you look for the secret stairway up to the highest tower in the castle. Should you find the way up, you must search for the correct key to open the lock. With key in hand, you may open the heavy door. Inside you see the child looking out the window. He does not turn to greet you. You may walk over, and being ever so careful not to speak to the child or even touch him, you may stand beside him and look out the window. After a while, you may speak, in quiet tones, about what you see when you look out the window.

If you have been careful and respectful enough and have noticed the "right" things as you looked out the window, the child may turn to acknowledge that he is no longer totally alone.

You will spend a long time in the tower, often longer than you imagined. Then a day may come when the child notices the door and leads you to it. You open the door. The child lets you hold his hand as you creep down the castle stairways, past the guards, out the door, across the moat and into the outside world. You will spend a long time exploring together. Maybe the day will come when the child, who has now grown older, says, "Farewell, I'm ready to explore with others and by myself."[1]

---

[1] A metaphor given by Pierre Johannet, M.D., to the nursery teachers at the James Jackson Putnam Children's Center, Roxbury, Massachusetts, between 1962 and 1967, as retold by Nancy Reiser to therapists she supervises and parents she sees. Nancy Reiser was the author's nursery school teacher at this center.

In the 1960s, given the child on the autism spectrum's insistence upon sameness along with an unawareness of the environment, autism was considered a psychological disorder. Consequently, these children were treated with utmost delicacy lest they erupt into a tantrum. While the causes of autism and Asperger Syndrome remain unknown, we now know that working *with* the child's resistance to change and lack of awareness is the crux of how to lead children on the autism spectrum towards more meaningful and successful lives.

A SLICE OF LIFE

.

CHAPTER ONE

A Slice of Life

I am awakened at 6:30 a.m. by a bluejay who has decided that it is time for everyone else to wake up too. It hurts. It feels like his beak is scraping against my eardrum. I close the window to catch another 30 minutes of sleep.

> I have strong sensitivities to sounds. When I was in grade school, my classmates used to call my name as softly as they could to see if I could still hear them – I could hear them from across the room and often even into an adjacent class-room. One time a teacher did something similar. He stood behind me and barely whispered my name. I still sensed his presence and looked around. The whole class, teacher included, had a good laugh.

> During the 1970s, as a holdover from the fears of the Cold War, a siren sounded at noon every Friday, causing many dogs to howl in unison. Sitting in class one Friday I copied the sound as it went off. I didn't become aware of it until I suddenly noticed the whole class laughing. Needless to say, I was embarrassed and my classmates made sure that I didn't forget that episode for a long time.

It is now time to get up. My wife and I arise and do the usual morning activities of preparing for the day and eating breakfast. Time to shave. No, I don't shave. Shaving feels like a power sander scraping my skin. As a result, I've had a beard almost from the time I first needed to shave. Using a razor hurt terribly. My parents asked me why I didn't want to shave my face, explaining to me that it was a male-type ritual. I told them it hurt. "Don't be ridiculous" was their response. An electric shaver is tolerable if I don't use it often and on only the small portions of my face that I don't want the beard to cover.

Still trying to get ready, I look for the day's clothes to wear. It doesn't matter what they are as long as the socks do not have holes in them or the fabric is weak so that I can see my toes or heel through it. Socks with holes or with thinning fabric are the biggest issues for me in terms of clothes. There is something profoundly upsetting about wearing such socks and I don't even like to see holes or weak areas on other people's socks. If I avert my eyes when putting on such socks, I may be able to tolerate them as long as I can't feel where the holes are, but that is usually not the case. Holes in an undershirt are only slightly more tolerable while holes in pants and other outerwear are not a problem. Newly purchased clothes have a disagreeable smell to me. So that new shirt, received as a gift, must wait until it has been washed before I can wear it.

When ready, I get on my bicycle and ride to work. Even though I got my driver's license and a car when I was 16 years old, I still prefer to ride my bicycle everywhere I go. Is this a stim? I don't know. I still like spinning objects, and a bicycle has many rotating parts. Sometimes my wife drops me off with my bicycle at the college where I teach, but I always ride home.

I call riding the bicycle to work the lazy man's way to get around. It takes 20 minutes by bicycle, the same amount of time by car and about an hour by public transportation, to get to work. I avoid public transportation whenever possible because it is often jam-packed with people, usually hot and quite smelly.

When I arrive at work, I lock up my bicycle, walk to my desk, change my shoes and pull on a sweater vest Mr. Rogers style. I get to school about two hours before my first class. This gives me time to get oriented, work on projects and visit with colleagues.

I call my friend Phyllis, the art professor. We exchange ritualistic greetings in Russian and agree to meet for tea at my office. We discuss our students. We both enjoy imitations and I am good at it so we spend the next half an hour imitating people we both know. Suddenly, an overpowering smell of perfume wafts from the office below mine. This olfactory assault is followed by the creaking of an opening door. The occupant of the office below me is ready to start her day. With my eyes watering, we decide to go to Phyllis' office.

Phyllis is a special friend. We have exchanged histories and we enjoy looking into each other's worlds. She is my age, within a few months. But unlike me, she appears to have had a fairly normal childhood. She enlightens me about all the "normal" childhood things.

After a while she goes to class, and I visit the dean of Business, whom I call my adopted dean. He is probably the most honest and straightforward man on the campus. Whether he knows it or not, I have designated him my mentor. I am very poor at reading subtle social situations. Office politics is full of that. This man helps me decode what is going on and how to act or not act.

The dean of Business doesn't know my personal history, and it wouldn't make sense to lay it all out for him. I suspect he sees me as a hard-working, interesting person who has much to offer to the college. He probably senses that I am "different" in some ways but that is about where it ends.

Before I got to know and trust this man the way I do, we had a falling out. I had approached him during his tenure as chair of the Business Department with an idea of developing a music business program at our college. He told me that while this was a great idea, it wouldn't work "… due to the fact that the Business Department was stretched to the maximum at this time, along with there being no budget for publicity." He is honest and hard-working, so I took him at his word and didn't think more of it. Later that week when my dean asked me to write a memo about my conversation about a music management program, I repeated the words of the Business chair verbatim. The memo was later forwarded to the vice president of academic affairs, who interpreted the statement as my saying that the chair of Business was lazy and had no energy to consider another program.

The Business Department chairman got angry with me and much yelling ensued. With the assistance of a friend of mine, the problem was cleared up and the chair of Business and I ended up becoming good friends.

It had never occurred to me that whatever I wrote to my dean would be repeated verbatim to somebody else and misinterpreted. The lesson for me is that all memos must be written as if anyone in the entire college might read them and that whenever there is a possibility that someone might look bad, special pains must be taken to prevent it.

After this latest visit with the dean of Business, it is time for electronic music class. Immediately, "prosopagnosia" (a fancy word for facial recognition problem) rears its ugly head as it does for every class I teach. To overcome this problem, I take attendance every day and look at everyone's face as they call out "here!" I then pass out homework. I call the names written on the homework and wait for a look of recognition or expectation of receiving homework. This tells me to whom the work belongs. If I misread this look or miss it, the homework gets passed out to the wrong person or not at all. When this happens, I get embarrassed. The techniques I use to help me with facial recognition don't seem to help much. But, I'd hate to see what would happen if I hadn't discovered this tool.

The difficulties in differentiating between similarities appear to be restricted to facial recognition. For example, determining variations in two or more examples of text or graphical formatting, music and other objects is easy and enjoyable. In examining text or graphical formatting, I seem to be able to catch what I term "formatting violations" without even reading the content of the text or determining what the graphic is about. Determining content seems to be secondary to finding these errors.

Often, I have felt an urge to disclose my relation to the autism spectrum to the dean of Business and to inform my students that facial recognition is difficult for me. However, the fear of being stigmatized stops me unless I have complete trust in the person I am revealing it to.

After teaching other classes during the day, I prepare to meet a friend for a musically oriented session with her son. Zachariah is five and a half years old, born with a hole between the chambers of his heart. Officially diagnosed as having Pervasive Development Disorder-Not Otherwise Specified (PDD-NOS), Zack also has apraxia[2] of speech. Individuals with autism have difficulty speaking due to the neural setup (or perhaps mis-setup) in their brain. In general, the pathways from the brain to the muscles for speech are intact. For Zack, however, these pathways are also miswired. As a result, speech will probably never be his primary mode of expressive communication. He is nonverbal, except for about five words. His father, I believe, is also somewhere on the autistic spectrum. When I first discussed this possibility with him, he was resistant to the idea. However, as time went on, and with more thinking and research into his own history, Zack's father has come to realize his own autistic tendencies. He now believes that at least he was on the autism spectrum as a child, if not still at the lighter end of the severity scale of this disorder.

---

[2] Apraxia refers to the loss or impairment of the ability to execute complex coordinated movements without impairment of the muscles or senses. In other words, the mechanics of speaking are present but the neural connections needed to do so are not.

My first meeting with Zack was fairly uneventful. I played the piano while his mother attempted to get him to beat time on the drums with drum sticks. Zack was on task for about 10 percent of the time we spent together.

Zack in his element as he naps on a couch.

The instruments I chose were a set of tom-toms and a cymbal. I decided against a snare drum as I felt it created too many complex high-pitched sounds. I was wary about the cymbal too but took the risk.

With the assistance of his mother, Zack would be on task 5-10 percent of the time. When Zack played, he beat the drums in a musically sensitive way. What he did with the cymbals was fascinating. Instead of bashing them with the sticks and making a horrendous sound, he gently scraped the drum stick across the cymbal to make a soft sound. It was as if he was consciously avoiding the loud sounds the cymbal could potentially make.

Zack communicated with his mother via a bracelet of small pictures she wore on her wrist. His frequent requests to go to the bathroom appeared to be an escape mechanism. Zack did not like it when I played the piano. He would remove my hands from the keys and perseverate on the first three white keys on the left. I figured, "OK Zack, you play the piano and I'll play the drums." So I'd go to the drums. But he would also remove my hands from the drums. According to mother, Zack didn't like anyone to play an instrument, not just me.

The three following meetings went in a similar fashion. There was not much real communication between Zack and me. It felt as if we were doing our own things, side by side, in the same room. Such parallel actions are a common trait of autistic play. I sensed that Zack had no idea of what I wanted him to do. Since he had no idea of the objectives of the session, he had no opportunity to figure out what he was to do.

Frustrated, I talked with his mother and as a result, we came up with the idea of using an activity board and a time board.

> The boards are made with corrugated cardboard rectangles about 4 inches high by 12 inches wide. Mayer-Johnson[3] pictures are then taped to oaktag squares about one and a half inches square. On the back of the oaktag squares are Velcro™ dots, which are stuck onto a Velcro™ strip on the board itself. A Velcro strip is also attached to the back of the board for storing additional activity pictures.
>
> Made in a similar manner as the activity board, the time board shows the numbers 1, 2, and 3, along with a sign of "all done." The activity board gives a visual representation of the activity. The time board allows the child to see the passage of time and know that the activity will come to an end.

---

[3] Mayer-Johnson. Pictures created by Mayer-Johnson used for nonverbal communication. Available: http://www.mayerjohnson.com or at Mayer-Johnson, Inc., P.O. Box 1579 Solana Beach, CA 92075-7579. Phone: 800 588-4548 or 858 550-0084.

Finally, an additional small square with the words "do this" is placed below the task pictures in order to get the child started on the task.

Before these tools could be used, the tasks Zack needed to do had to be broken down into tiny steps.

1. Pick up stick
2. Tap drum four times
3. Stop
4. Put down stick

Suddenly Zack understood! He demonstrated his ability to understand and do as I had asked. Mirroring what I did, he picked up the stick, tapped the drum four times, and put the stick down again. I communicated with Zack!! What enabled Zack to understand what I wanted from him? Here are the two important reasons.

1. A structure was built that he could understand. That is, the activity and time boards visually communicated to him exactly what was expected.

2. The tasks were broken down into something he could understand.

I had climbed up to the highest tower of the castle, and Zack, aware of my presence and meaning, had turned to look at me. Zack was very happy during that session, giving me hugs and generally showing great pleasure. There were also many fewer trips to the bathroom. As for all of us, when Zack understands what is expected of him and he can perform the task, he is happy. And his happiness is very infectious.

I credit this breakthrough in communication with Zack mostly to his mother, who came up with the idea of using the activity and time boards. Visually representing the activities allowed Zack to understand what activity we were about to do. The time board was important as it allowed Zack to see the passage of time so he did not have to wonder if he might be spending the rest of his life doing a particular task.

After my session with Zack, it is now about 4 p.m. and time to go home. It is raining but that doesn't matter. Riding home on my bicycle beats the alternative of smelly public transportation.

I get home at about 4:30, relaxed by my bicycle ride. My wife is already home and we greet with strong hugs and a kiss. As Chinese and American food is prepared for dinner, we discuss the events of the day. The routine of doing this adds predictability and stability to my day. Following an after-dinner nap, ranging from 10 minutes to one hour, I prepare for the next day's activities.

CHAPTER TWO

My Early Life

Pediatrician: We know he is not retarded ... but he may be autistic.
Let me think about it.

I was the third, and was to become the penultimate, of four children. But my parents' plan of having four children, spaced every two years, got derailed after I arrived, as they had to work with both the continual challenges of my mild to moderately retarded brother and now me. My sister, Robin, was born four years prior to me, and my brother Martin, two years after that. Previous to my birth, my parents rented a separate part of my maternal grandparents' home in Milton, Massachusetts. In preparation for continued children-rearing years and my arrival, they purchased a small home in a community that was originally built for temporary housing for World War II veterans in Newton, Massachusetts.

I was born on September 27, 1961, after only two hours labor. The late obstetrician/gynecologist Dr. Daniel Hindman at the Beth Israel Hospital in Boston handled the birth. Dr. Sidney Brodie, my pediatrician, did an in-hospital exam, which among other things revealed a high Apgar[4] of 9.

---

[4] The Apgar test is an index used to evaluate the condition of a newborn infant. It is based on a rating of 0, 1, or 2 for each of the five characteristics of color, heart rate, response to stimulation of the sole of the foot, muscle tone, and respiration, with 10 being a perfect score.

Here I am at 24 hours.

I was an "easy" infant, who shocked my family by turning over at eight days. I am told that I was very agile and noncompetitively athletic, as well as gentle and quiet. This holds true today, as I like bicycle riding and rock climbing. My sense of balance is good and I actually enjoy the challenge of riding on snow and ice while keeping upright on my bicycle.

Sports were always difficult during my public school years. I was never good at team contact sports. Baseball and softball were impossible. I could never hit the ball and until about age 10, I was afraid that the ball would hit me. My father must have sensed my fear, as he would roll grounders to my brother and me when the three of us played ball in the street. In elementary school, I was always one of the last people chosen for a team. It was too difficult for me to detect, interpret and follow through on all the social cues from my teammates.

Team sports continued to be difficult all through public school. In middle school I signed up for the 100 Mile Club, which meant running around a track with the goal of completing 100 miles by the end of the semester. I did well with this alternative activity. Running around a field was much easier for me because it was a solitary sport. Even running alongside my classmates was fine because success in this activity was not dependent on reading nonverbal cues and handling social interactions that eventually led to my being rejected by my classmates for not having the necessary motor coordination and muscle strength to contribute to the team. My mother often told me to join the neighborhood children in games of kickball down the street, but I responded with "I hate sports." My feelings of inadequacy in these team sports drove me away from participating in them.

Finally, at an overnight camp as a preteen, I learned to hit a ball with the bat. A kid would toss the ball to me and I could often get the bat to make contact with the ball from about 10 feet away. But the bat was very heavy and the ball never went far. One day, while in the outfield playing a game of softball, I managed to catch a ball. I saw it coming, put my hand out, and started focusing on the trees at the edge of the field. Suddenly the ball slammed into my glove. Fortunately, that represented the third and final out for the other team so I didn't have to do anything with the ball once it was in the glove. As the two teams switched positions on the field, a camp counselor told me that I needed to pay attention to the ball when I caught it. My arm and trunk muscles, along with poor coordination, were not strong enough to play baseball well.

I was introduced to rock climbing at this time by my sister's boyfriend and a teacher at school who ran a rock-climbing club. Rock climbing suited me well. The teacher asked me if I had ever rock-climbed before, as it seemed to come naturally to me. I answered that I must have been a rock climber in a former life.

Bicycling worked well for me too. In high school I did a lot of touring and joined a bicycle riding club. Bicycling was a great way to meet other people and there was always plenty to talk about. Instead of participating in gym in high school, I was allowed to draw up my own program, which involved training for bicycle races.

In undergraduate college a group of friends would get together to ride bicycles. One fellow and I often went on midnight rides. The only group gym-related course I signed up for was a yoga class, which I enjoyed greatly. Eastern medicine is something that I have been interested in since middle school. After graduating college and while working in a bank, I studied Shiatsu (acupuncture without the needles) for a year with much interest.

At the end of my student teaching practicum, my lack of knowledge about sports collided with having to keep score for a football game. My cooperating teacher, the principal of the school, and some other people and I were watching the school football game from an elevated box. My teacher was keeping score with a dial mechanism that communicated the score to a large scoreboard at the end of the field. To my horror, he suddenly looked at me and said, "You're the student teacher, why don't you keep score." All I knew about football was that there were two teams, each trying to get the ball from the middle of the field, through the other team, to the other end of the field. I turned to the principal and suggested that since it was his school, perhaps he might want to keep score. He refused and there was no escape.

For a while some outrageous scores showed up on the display board as I figured out what the numbers on the field meant and how many yards were gained along with keeping score. But nobody made any comments about the erroneous scores and numbers. By the end of the game I had figured it out and found it rather interesting.

Individual, noncontact sports worked the best. I could rely on myself to participate and wasn't dependent on reading or coordinating myself with other people's actions. Although rock climbing is very dependent on coordinating with other people, the commands are unequivocal and have single, specific meanings. Bicycle sports seem more dependent on doing what the body feels it needs to do in order to pull ahead, avoid crashing, etc., as opposed to the various ball-oriented games.

I still don't like to watch team, ball-oriented games as I find them boring. Sometimes people talk to me about these games and somehow I can't get them to understand that I am not interested. I deliberately, with a sense of humor, pretend to confuse local hockey, basketball, football and baseball teams and ask questions such as, "When are the Red Sox (baseball) and the Celtics (basketball) going to the playoffs for the Stanley Cup (hockey championship)."

A few months after I was born, my parents became concerned about my brother, Martin, who appeared to be developing more slowly than "normal." As a result, they took him to a pediatric neurologist when he was 25 months old. The report indicated the potential for mild to moderate mental retardation. The scary part was the doctor's suggestion that Martin be placed in a separate room of our home so as to isolate any destructive behaviors to a single location – a great recipe for turning a human into a monster. Later, vitamin E was recommended as a therapy for counteracting Martin's delays and destructive behaviors.

At approximately six months or even earlier, I began to make "talking" sounds and could say "mama." But shortly thereafter I stopped and seemed unhappy when taken from my crib. I must have considered my crib a safe haven. I would rock in my crib and loved using it as a trampoline while the family applauded my jumping. This was the only time for some years to come that the whole family would laugh together.

Ever since I became aware of what a trampoline was in elementary school, I have wanted one and still do. My desire for a trampoline was partially satisfied with a pogo stick. It never occurred to me to ask my parents for a trampoline. Often it does not occur to me that I have the power to change the focus of whatever I find upsetting. This can cause difficulties when things could be improved because I am trapped in the events of the situation.

For example, when my parents found out children were bullying me in school and I spent much time cowering with the lunch ladies, they asked me why I never told them about it. I just thought that was how school was supposed to be. Probably having someone present choices for different courses of action would have helped. Even to this day when offered a drink or food, I need to be given a list of alternatives as a structure to help make my selection. The underlying structure of options seems to be necessary for me to make a choice, but it does not occur to me to create one on my own.

I started walking at 10 months. Soon thereafter, I was often found with my finger in my ear turning around in circles. As I grew older, I enjoyed any lawn or playground toy that involved a spinning motion. My favorite was a four-seat carousel that spun like helicopter blades as the footrests and handles were alternately pushed and pulled. I must have been seeking vestibular stimulation. To this day I like spinning objects.

My mother had no answers to the questions that were gradually filling her head. But she knew there was something wrong with me. From observing Martin, she believed that retardation was not the problem. When my mother contacted our pediatrician with her concerns, he sat quietly, kind of troubled, and then said, "We know he is not retarded ... but he may be autistic. Let me think about it." Upon remembering this time my mother wrote:

> *When the pediatrician stated this, it verified my own belief that Stephen was not retarded. I didn't know much about autism, however, and so, in frustration over yet another problem I would be forced to carry alone, I wept. My husband did not then and never has had much understanding of or interest in cognitive, neurological, or psychiatric difficulties in humans. In fact, while this can*

create a very lonely place for me, it may well have a great upside as he appears to go through life treating his children unaware of their existing impairments and expecting normal behavior from them. My doctor was the one who comforted me.

CHAPTER THREE

Sinking into the Grip of Autism

After my first year, according to the E-2 Questionnaire,[5] I was unresponsive to bright lights, colors and unusual sounds, didn't anticipate being picked up by raising my arms, and rocked a lot in my crib. It was as if others couldn't reach me. Picking me up was not easy as I was stiff and awkward to hold. The E-2 noted that although I often appeared deaf, I did respond to low sounds. As an adult, I still like low-pitched sounds. Although there seemed to be problems with fine-motor control, it appeared that I was unusually agile. Finally, the form indicated that I often spoke in a peculiar voice tone, imitated whom I was speaking to and reversed pronouns. As a toddler, I would not kiss my father. The smell of coffee on his breath and the scratchiness of his moustache was too much for me to bear. Trying to help, my mother would ask, "Is there a problem? If you can tell us, we can fix it." But I couldn't find the words to tell her.

Haircuts were always a major event. They hurt! To try to calm me, my parents would say that hair is dead and has no feeling. It was impossible for me to communicate that the pulling on the scalp was causing the discomfort. Having someone else wash my hair was also a problem. Now that I am older and my nervous system has matured, a haircut is no longer an issue.

---

[5] Questionnaire developed by Dr. Bernard Rimland to acquire large amounts of data about children. The questionnaire was completed on me when I was 12 years old as part of a followup study on children with autistic tendencies conducted by the school I attended.

During my preteen and teen years I was aware of having a strong reaction to being touched unexpectedly. My response would be to jump slightly. My mother explained, "No one is going to hit you! Why do you jump?" I couldn't tell her. I didn't know why. This still happens to a small extent when, for example, my wife puts her hand on my knee while driving. I don't mention it and as far as I know she doesn't detect my discomfort. If I am prepared, usually by seeing the hand approaching, then I show no startled reaction to being touched.

When I was two years and two months old, my mother took my brother and me to Fernald School in Waltham, Massachusetts, for evaluation. Results read, in part, as follows.

> ... *Stephen is 2 years and 2 months old. On physical examination he is a good-looking youngster, who reacts in a passive way to the examiner. Height is 31 inches, weight 29 pounds and head circumference measures 49-1/2 centimeters. All figures are in the average normal range. There are no significant physical abnormalities. Posture and coordination appear normal. Muscle tone and tendon reflexes are within normal limits. No pathological reflexes are present. There is no speech. Hearing and vision are grossly normal.*

After discussing this extremely distressing situation with one of Martin's preschool teachers at the Greater Boston Association for Retarded Citizens, my mother was advised to get in touch with the James Jackson Putnam Center[6] in Roxbury for further evaluation. This was in the early part of 1964.

---

[6] The James Jackson Putnam Children's Center had a strong psychoanalytic bent. Founded in 1943 by Beata Rank, a psychiatrist, it was named after the father of the director.

At four years of age, my brother and I (left) in the pool with our maternal grandfather, whom we called Papa.

My official diagnosis from this center was "atypical development" in addition to "psychotic behaviors and strong autistic tendencies." This diagnosis was applied to a wide range of children they worked with, who fell outside of what they had defined as "normal" development. Today I would probably have been diagnosed with Pervasive Developmental Disorder-Not Otherwise Specified (PDD-NOS) or autism spectrum disorder.

Up until about four years of age, I was still mute and not eating anything but puréed baby food. In fact, I still have memories of my father feeding me baby food in the mornings.

In 1964 I began annual neurological workups, which included electroencephalograms (EEGs), at Massachusetts General Hospital by Boston's most eminent pediatric neurologist, Mary Louise Scholl, M.D. The EEGs were normal.

At age four, on the right, watermelon was one of the first things I ate. My brother is between my maternal grandmother and me.

According to my mother, when I was about three years old, I would stand in the backyard turning in circles with my finger in my ear. If my mother called to me, I didn't seem to hear. If she went over to me, touched me and said "Stephen …," I quickly took her hand and accompanied her into the kitchen for lunch. It was that bodily contact that allowed my mother to enter into my Umwelt,[7] or perception of the environment.

Around this time, my brother and I were at the swing set one day. Martin was sitting on a swing and I was hanging upside down on a metal support bar underneath the slide. We weren't playing together but just happened to be on the same piece of playground equipment.

Suddenly, I took flight and ran to the flagstone patio where my mother and several of her friends were drinking iced tea. Right in front of these women I stopped, got down on my knees and

*I am about two years old. My great aunt and uncle
are holding (from left to right) my brother Martin,
my sister Robin, and me. I would do anything
to escape from the loving clutches of my uncle.*

---

[7] German for the "world around one."

elbows, and whacked my forehead on the stones. I immediately started bleeding all over from the self-inflicted head wound, which caused emergency room treatment and stitches. Until recently my mother assumed this incident was caused by Martin, who could be aggressive although he rarely was. However, this fit of rage was caused by the freezing cold bars under the back of my knees. The cold was an insult to my body comfort.

Another picture of me (left) at about age three in the back yard of my maternal grandparents in Milton, Massachusetts. I appear uncomfortable in the group and within myself. My sister protectively holds me in order for the picture to be taken.

A few months later I was evaluated by the experts from Putnam, who informed my parents that I had strong autistic tendencies and was psychotic. They recommended that I be removed from a home with so much tension and a newly diagnosed retarded brother.

I have recently learned that my parents had an ally in support of rejecting the school director's recommendation of removal from my home at this time. This ally bluntly and directly stood up to the school director noting that he connected with me and saw much potential for improvement. The director later referred him to psychotherapy for coming up with such outlandish ideas of connecting with such an obviously disordered child, and most likely for insubordination as well. Eventually, this person had to move on.

Although he had much success in working and understanding children, his direct and blunt manner resulted in
the loss of many jobs as well as creating difficulties in
relating to other people. As a result, he began to wonder if he too might be on the autism spectrum. After further research,he found at the elderly age of 70 that he did
indeed have Asperger Syndrome. At one level, this finding is about circles closing and paths crossing. At another, deeper level, it is about one person connecting with
another of his own kind followed by voicing his recognition of value and humanity in another in a challenging
environment that is often not open to the potential of
those on the autism spectrum.

Thankfully, my mother is psychologically aware. To their suggestion of foster care, she sarcastically commented that it was
"wonderful" to know that psychologically oriented foster homes
existed. I remained at home. The staff agreed to admit me to
nursery school and therapy about a year later, even though they
felt I "was so sick."

My mother at this time was suffering from undiagnosed
agoraphobia, which is an atypical depression. Agoraphobia
translates to "fear of the market place" or "open spaces."
In extreme cases, individuals with this disorder are restricted to certain rooms of their home. My mother was able to
leave the house as long as it was still in sight. However,
walking to the supermarket down the street, out of sight of
the house, with the possibility of feeling trapped as she
waited in the cashier's line was often intolerable for her.

One time we were all in the car on the way to Nantasket
Beach for the day when my mother broke into tears and said
she couldn't continue any more and had to go home. We
went home. Being constrained to a very limited geographi-
cal area and unable to do what most people took for grant-

ed made my mother very unhappy. This unhappiness was incorrectly interpreted as depression being the primary cause of her problems. In fact, much of her sadness was fear that she was failing her children.

The challenge of living with undiagnosed agoraphobia combined with having two atypical young boys created a great obstacle for my mother and the family as a whole. But while my mother felt a great inadequacy regarding her functioning in the world outside of the home, she worked her hardest to do the best she could inside. By means of telephone conversations with a supportive social worker from the Beth Israel Hospital, my mother regained enough self-confidence to provide me with the badly needed early interventions during that yearlong waiting period for my admittance to the James Jackson Putnam Children's Center.

During that year Martin started preschool, so I was able to spend a lot of time with my mother while he was gone. Because she loved and needed classical music for her emotional well-being, our radio was always tuned to the local classical radio station. Mother hummed, sang and conducted the aural orchestra. Sometimes we played folk music such as James Taylor, Judy Collins, Seals & Crofts, and others. I never imitated her, but the experience must have had profound meaning for me, as I have a similar need for classical music. Mother also spent a lot of time talking and playing with me. Even though I didn't appear to be aware of her, she continued her efforts believing that, somehow, what she did was beneficial to me. This seemed to work as I slowly admitted her into my world.

Upon learning that I was working on this autobiography, my mother wrote the following.

Mother's Recollection of My Early Life

Born on his due date, after a quick two-hour labor, Stephen Mark Shore weighed 7 pounds, 3 ounces and got a 9 on his Apgar! My husband and I have three children and each developing fetus was different. Rather a glimpse into the future, I thought.

The first child, a girl, was very active. The second child, a boy, was even more active. Stephen had been a peaceful pregnancy. Whether this was due to my distraction by the other kids or his personality, I didn't yet know.

When he was laid in my arms, I thought "What a beautiful boy." He was blond, looked just like his father and was indeed peaceful, nursed well and then returned to sleep. He was extremely well developed physically – turning over in his crib in front of both my cousin and me following his ritual circumcision at eight days.

There was nothing remarkable about this period except that I was disturbed that I often found myself angrily shouting at our two-year-old. Our recently diagnosed disabled son would take advantage of my holding and nursing Steve by acting out. I worried that the baby would think I was yelling at him and wondered if there would be any long-term repercussions. After several months, this bothered me enough to wean him to a bottle so that his feeding times could be more calm. In retrospect, I might have been able to find someone to entertain Martin at that time. I felt very badly for Stephen, who exhibited so much early promise.

Emotionally, I was going through a private hell on two fronts. Though it had no name for many years – and I felt like a pariah – the agoraphobia of which I had had glimmers since childhood was coming into full bloom; our second child,

Martin, who was causing havoc in the house, was, as I had suspected, developmentally delayed. We had waited to have him tested as we had no idea what "normal" was. Robin had spoken in full sentences and walked by a year. Also nursed, she rejected baby food for table food from the beginning. She was a wonderful and entertaining baby. Martin was also wonderful, but as he became a toddler, the frustrations he had to deal with, such as lack of intelligible speech and poor motor development, meant that he cried and screamed almost the entire day. Respite came in the form of my mother, who took him to her house so she and my father could play with him all weekend. This went on for a year.

Also at this time, my husband was operating a single-person business, leaving the house by 8 a.m. and usually not coming home until near midnight. He was exhausted, short-tempered, and very frustrated about and with Martin.

At that time, the Department of Mental Health & Retardation was operated out of whatever state school was closest to your residence. As a result, all the testing of our children was done at Fernald until the rules changed and we sought assistance in the private sector.

That was a busy time. Continual fighting of anxiety attacks. Getting Robin started in kindergarten, and making connections with the Greater Boston Association for Retarded Citizens about a preschool nursery, where Martin and I could get a break from each other every day. Looking back I don't really know how I survived. It is a good thing, I believe, that I have never cared for alcohol!

While we now know about agoraphobia, I was at that time very depressed. My well-meaning physician kept giving me various medications such as Miltown, Tofranil, Librium (at different times, of course) to try to alleviate what he observed as a terrible situation. Throughout these years, I sometimes felt like a caretaker instead of a mother to my boys. I now realize that it was a defense and a way to deal with our problems in a clinical, nonemotional way. Often I felt I got what I deserved and that Robin was short-changed having a mother like me. Perhaps she felt that way as well. She later spent long years seeking a surrogate mother, telling me about it, and criticizing our family values. Ultimately, she rejected them. All of these mother-daughter conflicts have now been resolved, for which we are both grateful.

Stephen had developed normally until he was a little more than a year old. He had started to talk and was relatively responsive – not hyper like Martin nor well integrated like Robin. He was indeed "The Quiet One" both before and after birth.

Once I had Stephen to myself, things got much easier. I never left a baby home alone, so each time I drove Martin to school, I would put Steve in the car also. His pattern was to act unhappy except when eating, if he was anywhere but in his crib. Eventually a baby-seat walker worked, but he never looked happy unless he was in bed. There he would croon, babble, and show wonderful physical abilities. Sometimes his brother climbed into the crib where they played nicely together.

Without any traumatic event to point to, somewhere in the first half of his second year, Steve stopped talking. As mentioned, he preferred his crib to anywhere else, even to the point of screaming when I would place him in the baby swing in the back yard, where other children and mothers were gathered. Although none of us (all the mothers) had ever seen such behavior, as a liberal-thinking group, we felt that since he could see the yard from his crib, there was no need to make Steve unhappy by forcing him to be outside. But it did make me uneasy.

To try to bring Steve out, I decided to verbalize everything. I talked to him in the car, at the table, in his room. He didn't appear to be hearing me, but I knew he was. On occasion I would speak nonsense or make a silly remark such as, "Look at that dog climb the tree," to which he would respond with a small, amused look at me from the corner of his eyes. He was musically aware too. I usually had music on and Steve would move to the tempo.

It seemed like the rudimentary sounds he was making were oddly like Martin's defective speech. As a retarded child with cerebral palsy, there were many sounds Martin could not make while others were garbled. Steve was copying him. I told him he didn't have to talk like his brother but he must have thought otherwise. Who knew about echolalia? I just said that people didn't have to do what parrots did.

During the times when we were alone, I admit that I some-times let Steve remain in the crib he loved so much because I was totally exhausted. Most of the time, however, I kept him at my side. He would always follow if offered a hand. When he made peculiar sounds or spoke in garbled words, I copied him. Slowly he began to acknowledge this and added the sounds of machinery, appliances, and animals to his vocabulary. He still is very talented at imitating things and people.

Not uncommonly, Martin would frustrate Steve, at which times instead of acting out, Steve became self-destruc-tive. Oh my, the pain of the child, the grief of the mother. He became a head banger and often banged against the wall from his bed after being put to sleep. In the beginning I would go in and resettle him. Months later, in weariness, I just rapped on the door to his room and said "stop that."

When Steve began head banging in frustration, we had to intensify our watchfulness. We never knew when he might do it and there was continual tension to make sure Martin was not a catalyst. In photographs of the kids taken around this time, Steve looks unhappy and spaced out. Sometimes I went into his room just to look at him in his sleep. At rest, he was still a beautiful, peaceful child. We needed help. My husband was rarely home and when he was, the whole situation confused him.

I sought and located the assistance needed to continue working therapeutically with Steve. Marta Abramovitz from the Putnam Children's Center in Roxbury was the catalyst to the future for me. From my first phone call and her sweet, Viennese-accented "How may I help you?," her caring words and tone caused me to weep. A year passed between evaluation and Steve's entry into their therapeutic nursery program. Because I now believed there was help ahead, I found the strength to carry on, working hard to help Stephen develop into the dear, puckish, sensitive man he is today.

Understanding the child's functioning level is vital to working with children on the autistic spectrum. If the child can't perceive or understand what the person working with him or her is doing, there is no hope of establishing meaningful communication. One of the children I worked with as a volunteer at the Language and Cognitive Development Center was named John Weissenberg. Often his behavioral problems made him difficult to reach. He had several stim routines some of which could be fairly elaborate. One day, while working with him on an elevated board structure,[8] he

---

[8] Developed to enhance body awareness and increase focused attention, they are systematically used at the Language and Cognitive Development Center in Jamaica Plain, Massachusetts.

was flicking his forefinger and thumb back and forth while making a clicking sound with his mouth in rhythm to the stim. I got right into his face about 2 inches away and imitated the stim back to him.

A huge smile spread across John's face and he opened right up. We did a lot of good work that day.

Although my mother had started making inroads towards helping me become aware of the environment and developing meaningful communication, there was much work to be done. I was terrified of going into the supermarket, for example; there was too much sound, too many people and vendors offering tasty but unwanted food. There were temper tantrums, too. I remember sitting at the curb at the end of my driveway smashing small rocks with a larger rock. Why? I was fascinated with the shiny, speckled bits of quartz inside these little stones. I did this for hours on end. This fascination with the inside of stones grew into acquiring a large rock collection, which had to be lined up in perfect order, and eventually into an intense interest in geology and geography. Special interests of great intensity have continued throughout my life. Usually I would have one interest at a time, sometimes two. Occasionally, specific interests would return. Some of these special interests were, and in some cases still are, as follows:

airplanes	astronomy	bicycles	earthquakes
medicine	chemistry	mechanics	electricity
electronics	computers	hardware	tools
psychology	music	rocks	geology
geography	locks	cats	dinosaurs
watches	shiatsu	yoga	autism

CHAPTER FOUR

The Putnam Period

A t age four, in the fall of 1965, I entered Putnam's nurs-
ery/therapy program. According to my nursery school
teacher, I had some verbal skills but was unable to make
my likes and dislikes known. In the year between evaluation and
nursery school I had been toilet trained but would still only eat
baby food. Thirty-three years later, my teacher remembered that I
was a neat and contained child with well-matched clothes.

As I mentioned earlier, the Putnam Center had a strong psychoanalytic bent. Teachers were not allowed to discuss the child's
progress in class to the parents based on management's belief that
nursery school teachers did not have sufficient training in psychoanalysis to properly interpret parental statements or questions.
For example, they were afraid that a mother's simple query into
whether her child ate lunch on any given day could be interpreted
as her questioning if the teacher was a better mother for the child
than she herself was. The directors meant well, but the children,
teachers, and the school as a whole missed out on valuable
parental input. Parents are the experts about their own child and
their input and assistance are not to be underestimated. When
talking with my nursery school teacher about this some 30 years
after she had worked with me, she wanted to make sure that I told
my mother that she felt badly about this and sent her apologies.
My mother is still irritated about the condescending policy of not
sharing information about the child's development and responded,

"The all-knowing doctors thought they had all the answers! Some, particularly the Freudians, held us responsible for our children's disabilities."

It was the belief of one of the co-founders of the Putnam Center that the main source of problems for the child with autism was "the tenuous relationship with an emotionally disturbed mother" (Rank, 1949, p. 136). The mother was thought of as an inadequate woman in whom "the sunshine which is radiated by the tenderly devoted mother is missing" (p. 132). This unfortunate parent of the child was assumed to be "a parasite so lacking in vitality that, vampire-like, they were stealing it from someone else" (Dolnick, 1998, p. 191). The mother wants a passive child "because he does not make exaggerated demands on the mother, who constantly feels in danger of revealing that emotionally she has nothing or little to offer, that she is a fraud" (Rank, 1949, p. 132).

The Classroom

There were a total of four kids in my classroom – David, Paul, Robertito, and myself. My most vivid memory of David is of the blue veins in his cheek and that he referred to urinating as "making a tinkle." To this day, I have a knack for remembering small and seemingly unimportant characteristics of objects and people.

The four children in the room had different traits. Paul had the ability to emote along with the capacity to experience and share feelings. David could talk; I was able to play; and Robertito was seen "as the baby you all once were."

As Nancy, my former nursery school teacher, reviewed the draft of this book, she wrote the following as part of her commentary.

> *... There were four children who together had the traits of one regular child. One had verbal language; one openly expressed feelings of distress, excitement, and anger; one had play skills; and [then there] was "The baby," who was relatively unreachable but present.*

My thinking then was rather inexperienced, but it felt to me that I could connect with Paul's feelings on behalf of all four children, that I could ask a question and David could answer and that you [Steve] had play skills that I could join and bring the others along. Robertito occasionally would let me hold him – my memory is that you three noticed this.

I'm not saying it well enough, I fear, but I recall that I could say, "David, look, Stephen has made a train. Here is a car for you to put on the track – or let's make a track for you also." Or "Paul is sooo unhappy today. He is crying. Boys cry when they have big sad feelings." In other words, I could use each of your obvious skills to speak to common issues/concerns – or just the moment. (personal communication, 1999)

The train tracks and trains were my favorite toys. I remember a period of time at home when the entire living room floor was taken up with a Lionel train set. I spent many hours watching the trains travel the tracks. At the Putnam Center, I connected curved lengths of track to run the train on. Paul and Dave could often be encouraged to link up tracks in a manner of playing along beside me but not really with me.

As mentioned earlier, I have always had very strong tendencies to imitate. This often results in my taking on others' speech, movement and sometimes emotional characteristics when I am in their presence without realizing it at first. I have clear memories of imitating my brother when I learned how to talk. Martin pronounced "daddy" as "dada," and so did I. This is how I thought people were supposed to talk. My parents would tell me that I didn't need to copy my brother but it took some time before I understood. Perhaps I had difficulty seeing myself as an autonomous being separate and distinct from my brother.

During my elementary through high school days, Martin and I often played an imitative word routine that could be initiated by either one of us. The reciprocity of the routine still feels good to go through with him. It went like this:

Stephen	*I am part of both boys.*
Martin	*I am part of both boys.*
Stephen	*Whatever one boy does.*
Martin	*Whatever one boy does.*
Stephen	*the other boy does too.*
Martin	*the other boy does too.*
Stephen	*When one boy sleeps in his bed.*
Martin	*When one boy sleeps in his bed.*
Stephen	*the other boy sleeps in his bed.*
Martin	*the other boy sleeps in his bed.*
Stephen	*When one boy goes to Nanny's house.*
Martin	*When one boy goes to Nanny's house.*
Stephen	*the other boy goes to Nanny's house.*
Martin	*the other boy goes to Nanny's house.*

Pronouns were not used. The routine would go on like this for other activities, too. Later this script evolved into us doing different activities such as:

Stephen	*When one boy goes to Nanny's house.*
Martin	*When one boy goes to Nanny's house.*
Stephen	*the other boy stays home.*
Martin	*the other boy stays home.*

Before speaking on my own, I went through a period of echolalia, which I don't remember.

The echolalic imitations I do of people's speech patterns can be embarrassing when I speak to people with accents, because I wonder if they realize that I am imitating them. During part of my tenure as a music instructor at a college, I would spend much time with the president's assistant. Many times I caught myself in horrified realization that I was talking like him to his face, copying his intonation and speaking style. He called me a homie so I'd refer to him as one. The word "homie" is used by African-Americans as a term of friendship or closeness. If he referred to me as a "brother," I would automatically do the same. But I would immediately stop and I never knew if he perceived my imitation.

Perhaps as an offshoot of echolalia, I also find myself imitating people's movements (echopraxia) and even emotions (echoemotica). Often I will pick up mannerisms of others when I am with them. One time I was told that this was due to a weakness in being able to form a personality. I think it is more a problem in separating oneself from the environment as a distinct and separate entity.

Whenever I get a very strong emotion and I am not clear as to where it comes from, I have to consider whether someone I am in communication with is displaying a similar emotion, which I am picking up from them. Sometimes I feel as if I am fused with that other person's emotions and can't separate myself.

One time when I was talking with my mother on the phone while at college, I got an overwhelming feeling of blackness when I talked to her and became very sad. Thinking about this, I realized that I didn't have anything to be terribly sad about and perhaps I had fused myself with an emotion from her. I called my mother back and found out that she was indeed terribly sad.

A similar thing happened towards the end of my undergraduate years while I was at my girlfriend's house one day and wondered why she didn't want to talk to me. She said, "My father is sick; I am upset and you don't want to talk to me." Prior to this statement I was feeling upset and not wanting to talk but I had no idea why. Her verbalizing the feelings cleared it up for me.

During my grade school years my mother would often ask me, "Who are you imitating?" On occasion I could determine whom I was copying, but most of the time I was not able to.

Another evaluation by the James Jackson Putnam Children's Center on my brother and me was completed when I was four and a half. After spending six months at the Center, I had graduated from being "atypical," autistic, and psychotic to merely "neurotic." As reported,

> ... However, during the one year that the family was on our waiting list for treatment, Stephen made rather remarkable progress and also in this year of treatment his progress has been exceptional. It seems as if his major difficulty was around issues of self-object differentiation and separating from his mother and functioning as an autonomous human being.
>
> This seems to be the area in which Stephen gained the most in the course of this treatment year, and presently he is functioning much more like a neurotic child than a psychotic child.

CHAPTER FIVE

Nursery School

Towards the end of my time at Putnam and after I had left, I went to a nursery school in Brighton at the Jewish Community Center. I don't have too many memories of that place except for playing outside on a tricycle with a television advertisement running through my head, using the bathroom, and making friends with a girl named Karen Sapers. I remember going to Karen's house and playing with her stuffed toys. There is also a memory of hitting her in the station wagon that took us home every day from the nursery school. She cried when I hit her. I think it may have been the reaction I was after, because she was my friend and I remember no negative thoughts or feelings towards her. My parents spent a lot of time asking me why I hit her, but I had no answer.

I also remember a classmate named Alison. If I poked my finger in her stomach, she would say "don't" in an elongated way, which I thought was pretty neat. Since my verbal skills were not developed to a point where I could easily interact with others, perhaps these two instances of challenging behaviors were a way for me to communicate with these children.

As I work with children on the autism spectrum, it has become clear to me that many challenging behaviors are a result of an inability to interact with the environment in a manner that is sensible to them. On the surface, challenging behavior is often thought of as noncompliance. An additional component is that it may be difficult to get the child "back on track" with the planned activity. Finding the source of the behavior via an understanding of how the child perceives the environment is key, as merely punishing for the behavior doesn't remove its cause.

1. Failure to comprehend a change or transition in the environment:

Close attention needs to be paid to transitions, and they must be prepared properly. Whereas most typical people can prepare for an upcoming change in their heads, often without conscious thought, those on the autism spectrum need preparation to come from an external source such as a teacher narrating an upcoming change in activity or talking through the change. Picture schedules can help greatly.

2. Frustration at not being able to communicate wants and needs:

Finding another mode of communication can help. Often verbal communication is difficult. However, it is better to work with the person's strengths, which often are visual. Communication boards and sign language are often better paths to communication and commonly serve as a bridge to verbal communication.

3. Sensory overload:

A commonly held theory is that people with autism have too many underdeveloped nerve endings. That is, the autistic behavior is a secondary result of the brain protecting itself from the overload of sensations. The brain learns how to shut down the offending senses as needed. Donna

Williams (1992), for example, can attend to only one sense at a time. Temple Grandin gets flooded with adrenaline when she hears high-pitched sounds (1995).

There was a child with autism who, upon entering the gym for a physical education class, would promptly throw up. Told that this behavior was inappropriate, the child would be put into time-out in order to give him time to calm down and think about what he did wrong. What actually happened is that the child had unintentionally trained his teachers to remove him from the gym class.

Looking at the situation from the child's point of view would have engendered better understanding. The child probably had an oversensitivity to sound. A gym is a noisy place with lots of echoes. Maybe supplying him with a set of head-phones or an alternate activity for physical education would have helped. Maybe there were physical education activi-ties that overwhelmed a too sensitive sense of touch.

Being aware of and dealing with these issues can reduce challenging behavior greatly. Of course, this is so much easier said than done.

Building blocks made of wood and a set of red toy bricks some-what like Legos were very important to me at this time. I spent long periods of time in the playroom constructing complicated and very tall structures. One of my favorite activities was to create structures with wooden blocks that were wedged between door-jambs. Woe be unto he or she who removed these structures.

Later, after I had received Legos as a gift, I often built two-story house trailers. Other structures were always replicas of buildings that I knew of such as the home I lived in, my grandparents' home, a friend's house, and so on. It never occurred to me to be creative and make up buildings. The Legos were red and white so any structures built from them had to have alternating red and white layers. Red was always the bottom layer. Red was my favorite color at that time. One time I remember having a tantrum and hitting my brother because he smashed one of these structures when I left the room. My parents dragged me into a cold shower, which stopped the tantrum. In addition, they spoke to Martin about what he had done.

Around this time, a second floor was added to our house as we needed more space. I was fascinated by the work, but was taken away to my grandparents' house for part of the construction. I wanted to stay but couldn't find the words to communicate it. One time my mother tried to carry me up the unfinished stairs to look at the skeleton that was to become living space. All I could see was an unfinished window and I felt scared at being so dangerously high up. I screamed in fear and we never made it more than halfway up the stairs. Although I was deeply interested in how the second floor was being built, getting close to and seeing the unfinished structure was disturbing to me.

The discovery of rubber bands was a real find. Few things were better for me at this age than making a chain of rubber bands to stretch throughout the house from the first floor to the second. I remember being incredibly impressed with the fact that one object made by me could stretch from one end of the house to the other. Perhaps the long chain of rubber bands served to remind me that while I was in one part of the house, another part that was attached to the other end of the chain still existed.

I was quite fond of taking long soaks in the bathtub. Often, my requests to take a bath were turned down because they took too much time. I would argue with my parents that the 30 or so minutes they allocated for my bath were not enough. Soaking and playing in a tub of warm, soapy water was very relaxing.

I was afraid of dogs because of their relatively unpredictable habits of barking and licking my face. Kittens, however, were quiet, didn't make loud noises and never slobbered my face. Often,

I would pretend to be a kitten whenever a bunch of children got together to play house. I remember going with my parents to pick up a puppy from a farm where they were giving away a puppy. I vehemently proclaimed that he was "their dog," not "my dog," and was not enthusiastic about bringing the dog home. His name was Kippy … because my brother could not pronounce the name "Skippy," which my parents had originally planned for the dog. Gradually, Kippy and I became friends and I learned not to fear dogs, which was my parents' original intent in getting one.

Age five or six with Kippy.

Thunderstorms, the moon, and fireworks all produced fear. The flash of lightening along with the accompanying thunder was too much of a sensory overload. One year when my family went to a fireworks display, we sat close to the front. I had a good time running around and watching my sister dance to rock and roll music – until the fireworks began. I was terrified of the sound and feared that the display produced by the rockets would float down and burn us. Assurance by mother that I wouldn't get hurt wasn't good enough. We finally left the lawn and watched the rest of the show from the car. The next year we watched the fireworks from an even safer distance – at home through a bedroom window.

Some time during my primary school days I somehow lost the fear of fireworks and thunderstorms and, now, I actually enjoy them. Perhaps this was a result of my increasing ability to admit less predictable events into my world.

Until the age of five or six, I couldn't stand anything wet linger-
ing on my face or hands. As a result, my face and hands had to be
Messy food was intolerable.
ade a royal mess of myself

food sensory

existed too. Brown or
black food wouldn't be
eaten as I insisted that

*Eating barbecued chicken
wings at age five or six.*

they were poisonous. Canned asparagus was intolerable due to its
slimy texture, and I didn't eat tomatoes for a year after a cherry
tomato had burst in my mouth while I was eating it. The sensory
stimulation of having that small piece of fruit explode in my
mouth was too much to bear and I was not going to take any
chances of that happening again.

Carrots in a green salad and celery in tuna fish salad are still
intolerable to me because the contrast in texture between carrots
or celery and salad or tuna fish is too great. However, I enjoy eating celery and baby carrots by themselves. Often as a child, less
now, I would eat things serially, finishing one item on the plate
before going on to the next.

Issues with uneven sensory input extended to other activities
too. One of these activities was learning to ride a bicycle. I had
difficulty learning to ride on the street, so my parents put me and

the bicycle on the grass in the front yard. Probably they felt I was afraid of getting hurt from falling. It worked. I could now ride on the grass but not the street. The bumpiness of the lawn may have forced me to be more aware of my body, which in turn enabled me to keep balanced on the bicycle. By six years of age, I had learned to ride on smooth pavement. Bicycles eventually became one of my many special interests.

I have always liked climbing trees. I was especially fond of a maple tree in our yard that I would climb to the height of the second-story window and sit there for extended periods of time. Often I climbed a particularly tall tree in my neighborhood to the height of about 40 feet, where the trunk was about 2 inches thick. Hanging on, I would look down on the tops of the telephone posts as the tree and I swayed in an arc of 7 to 10 feet. Although I knew the top wouldn't break off, I would remain there, swinging, utterly terrified. It made me feel more aware of myself in relation to the space around me. My brother sometimes joined me in climbing that tree.

My first "grownup" bicycle. It was purchased with the help of "Papa" after a long period of saving up money to buy it.

A family picture with my parents in the back and Martin next to me.

One day he fell off from a height of about 20 feet. Although he was OK, I nevertheless stopped climbing the tree after that. Perhaps it was the "edge experience" (Miller & Eller-Miller, 1973) I was looking for. Maybe it's the same thing people look for when they skydive?

As an elementary student I learned the wonders of the swing set. I would pump the swing as high as I could and jump off at a specific, calculated time. Jumping off too low and too soon resulted in getting catapulted forward, whereas launching off the swing too late resulted in a painful landing on my feet. Choosing the sweet spot between the two, however, resulted in a long arc with a smooth landing.

During my bicycle special-interest phase in middle and high school, I pedaled my bicycle as fast as I could into snow banks in order to enjoy the feeling of flight as I launched over the handlebars – and the thud of returning to earth on the snow. Later on, as I prepared for a bicycle trip to Montreal with an American Youth Hostel group, I learned how to jump both wheels of the bicycle at the same time. I now was able to jump over holes, railroad tracks and occasionally up curbs.

In retrospect, the commonality of swaying in the tree, jumping off the swing, and catapulting over the handlebars may have to do with body awareness. Activities that involved undergoing the peril of being at high elevation or being in flight seemed to increase my body awareness. The swing and the catapulting also resulted in a sudden stopping of motion, which increases body awareness as differentiated from the environment (Miller & Eller-Miller, 1989).

Accommodating Sensory Sensitivities

People on the autism spectrum often have issues with sensory integration. "Sensory integration is the neurological process of organizing the information we get from our bodies and from the world around us for use in daily life" (Kranowitz, 1998, p. 42). According to Dr. Ayres, the founder of sensory integration theory, "Over 80 percent of the nervous system is involved in processing or organizing sensory input, and thus the brain is primarily a sensory processing machine" (Kranowitz, 1998, p. 42). The brain and central nervous system modulate this input, which in turn

I was very proud to show off this large hole I had dug at the beach. Digging holes in the sand was quite a passion. I loved to make tunnels. I also made tunnels in snow banks during the winter that I could crawl through.

guides our physical, mental or emotional activity level. In people with autism, some or all of the five outer as well as the inner senses seem to be affected with hyper- or hypo-sensitivities to stimulation. In other words, some of the senses are turned up too high and create an overload whereas others receive information from the environment at too low a level to be perceived (Bundy & Murray, 2002). In addition, the information received may be distorted, full of "static," or otherwise unreliable in individuals who have autism spectrum disorders, which may play a large role in causing the developmental delays. Finally, sensory issues may help explain why people on the autism spectrum resist change. That is, it is easier to follow a known routine that requires little new input from the environment than to depend on new information received from an imperfect sensory system.

Outer and Inner Senses

The Outer Senses

Most people are aware of the five outer senses of touch, hearing, taste, smell, and touch. Temple Grandin (1995) and John Ratey (2001) have suggested a theory that people on the autism spectrum are born with too many, yet immature nerve endings. This theory possibly explains why most people with autism spectrum disorders experience problems with sensory integration. Some common examples include the following.

COMMON SENSORY REACTIONS

Sense	Possible Sensitivity	What it Feels Like	Common Reaction
Sight	Fluorescent lights	The 60 Hz cycling of the lights is visible. Feels like sitting in a room with a strobe light.	Child may try to escape or have a tantrum.
Sound	Birds tweeting	Feels like birds' beaks scraping the eardrum.	Child may cover his ears.
Taste	Avoidance of strong tasting food	Tasting like acid or some other extremely strong taste.	Child may spit food out.
Smell	Perfume	Feels like taking a deep breath from a Clorox bottle.	Sneezing, burning eyes, other allergic-like reactions. Child may try to escape.
Touch	Light touch	May feel like touching an open wound or getting an electric shock. May be overalerting.	Sensory defensiveness, brushing away light touch, jumping excessively at unexpected touch, seeking deep pressure.

The Inner Senses

The vestibular and proprioceptive senses are often referred to as the hidden or inner senses. The vestibular sense "helps with movement, posture, vision, balance, and coordination of both sides of the body" (Myles, Cook, Miller, Rinner, & Robbins, 2000, p. 28). Proprioception informs us of where our body parts are in space and the amount of force needed to perform an activity such as picking up a glass of milk. As with the more commonly known outer senses, hyper- and hypo-sensitivities as well as distortions of these two, inner senses cause challenges for those on the autism spectrum.

COMMON SENSORY REACTIONS

Sense	Possible Sensitivity	What It Feels Like	Common Reaction
Vestibular	"Low tolerance for activities involving movement" (Myles, et al., 2000, p. 29).	How most people would feel after spinning around at high speeds for a while. Dizziness or a lightheaded feeling.	Avoidance of any movement involving sharp changes in direction or the feet leaving the ground. Clumsy at team-oriented sports.
	Seeking vestibular stimulation.	Losing oneself in space: loss of coordination.	Attracted to roller coasters and similar amusement park rides.
Proprioceptive	Clumsy movements. Acts like "a bull in a china shop."	Having a body made of molasses. Movement is tiring.	Child often appears fatigued. Difficulty in modulating muscular force in everyday activities.

It is important to remember that we all have sensory integration problems at times. "It is when the brain is so disorganized that a person has difficulty functioning in daily life that the person is diagnosed with Sensory Integration Dysfunction" (Kranowitz, 1998, p. 26). The same holds true for autistic tendencies. In other words, most people experience autistic traits at one time or another.

It is when these traits are strong and numerous enough to significantly impact daily functioning that an autism spectrum diagnosis needs to be strongly considered.

Imagining that one's senses are 1,000 times more sensitive than reality can help a person to design environmental accommodations for those on the autism spectrum. Considering each sense individually can assist with organization of both the issues caused by the sensitivity and the remedies for relief. In considering the sense of sight, a

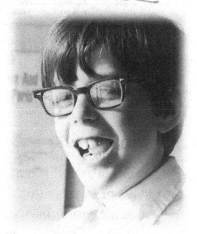

Here I am about nine years old. Photo taken at my great-uncle's house.

person with a vision hyperacuity might be bothered by the presence of fluorescent lights, because the lights cycle on and off 60 times per second in timing with the Hertz of alternating current. In such cases, a different form of illumination should be used. It is also possible that the humming from the ballast of a fluorescent lamp is irritating to individuals who are sensitive to sound.

> This point was driven home for me as I went into a library with a friend of mine who is on the autism spectrum. Suddenly, I noticed that her eyes were vibrating back and forth very rapidly. After a few seconds she asked me if we could leave the room. Realizing that her eyes were mov-

ing in synchronicity with the alternating current cycling through the fluorescent lights, I immediately agreed to leave the room.

The League School for Autism of Greater Boston was in the enviable position of being able to take such light sensitivity into consideration when they recently moved to a new location. In their new building they installed incandescent lighting in the classrooms, even though this resulted in a greater expense. The initial plan of using this type of lighting in the common areas of the school had to be abandoned, however, due to the prohibitive costs involved.

I find that becoming overstimulated from spending too much time on airplanes and sometimes at autism conferences often negatively affects my vestibular, proprioceptive, hearing, and other senses. However, swinging in a suspended hammock calms my senses and allows me to interact more effectively with the environment. In fact, during conferences I can often be found at the Playaway Toys display booth (www.playawaytoy.com) reorganizing my senses. Also, one of their hammocks is permanently wedged between the door jams of my home for use at any time I feel the need.

CHAPTER SIX

The Wonder and Terror of School

A t age six I entered a public school kindergarten, a year late, as a regular student. My first day in kindergarten was uneventful. After school I was surprised to see my mother waiting for me by the bushes near our home, anxious to hear how the day had gone – nothing major to relate. But soon I found that academics were difficult for me and things were a disaster for me on a social level. Children perceive differences very readily and will blatantly persecute classmates who seem "different." For me, this resulted in much teasing and unpleasantness. I lived in terrible fear of getting "beat up" at the end of every school day.

The teachers also thought I was strange. I was. I remember my third-grade teacher often telling me that I acted babyish. At the end of the year when she asked me how I felt about myself during that school year, I just repeated her words back to her as I thought this would make her happy. I was usually behind in math and reading by at least half a grade. The first-grade teacher said that I would never be able to do math. Nevertheless, somehow I learned and have even taught the subject at the college level. I believe this teacher would be shocked to learn that I went on to study calculus and statistics in college.

Sounds were and are still important to me. I had a repertoire of strange sounds and sayings that I repeated incessantly. Starting in kindergarten, for a period of time I would say the letter "B" over and over. I thought it was an ugly sound but I felt compelled to repeat it. When kids asked me to stop, I wouldn't. Unable to make me stop producing this sound, my classmates stopped associating with me and went about their school activities without me. In retrospect, perhaps this behavior was the root of kids making fun of me and bullying. However, it was impossible for me to draw a connection between the sounds and my classmates' reactions at that time. Some of the sound effects included "Whooooo, " with the "oo's" pronounced like the double "oo" in the word "look" and strung out like a siren. Growling sounds, along with wrinkling the nose and making a face like one had eaten an incredibly sour lemon, were all picked up from Andrew, the new dog my family had acquired. Some of the other students would also adopt these sounds and faces. This familiar repertoire of actions provided me with a comfortable, predictable way of interacting with the other children.

> In college, the sound of a classmate saying the word "auditing" in a New York accent resounded through my head for about a year. Today, I often greet people I know with repeated ritualistic sayings, and I give people what I think are interesting names such as Turtle Woman or Mushroom. These names often pick out a physical or personality characteristic, or the nickname may relate to how the person's name is spelled or pronounced. These playful names are not meant to be derogatory; they are cues that help me remember people's names.

First grade was when I began to fear other students. Because of some of my idiosyncratic behaviors, there was much unpleasantness and threats by classmates of beating me up after school every day. As a result, I often waited until everyone had left before summoning up the courage to run all the way home from school via an alternate route while keeping a sharp eye out for enemies. Recess was also a nightmare, as I clung to the lunch ladies in fear of other children. In third grade a kindly lunch lady told me that if I didn't appear to be nervously watching the other children, they probably wouldn't notice me and I might be able to enjoy recess more. That suggestion actually worked fairly well.

In second grade, the teacher remarked to my parents that I didn't know how to read and that something had to be done. My parents were taken aback at this comment as they had seen me read the newspaper at home. I remember reading the paper at an early age. I don't know how much I comprehended but I liked reading it. I liked the way it looked, particularly the *St. Petersburg Times*. That may have stemmed from hyperlexia.

> Often I enjoy looking at documents just for their look without paying attention to content. Formatting of documents is very important to me and I often move objects in increments as small as a single pixel (1/72 of an inch) on the computer screen until they look right.
>
> I also like the feeling of running my fingers over ink and graphics on a page of a book. Whenever I study a facsimile of a music score, I experience an overwhelmingly strong urge to feel the page with my fingers.

On occasion, the teasing from my classmates got to be too much, resulting in a meltdown. But often I left the classroom before this happened. I would wander from bathroom to bathroom until I felt like I could return to class. The teachers never seemed to make a big deal of this. But after one of these episodes, the third-grade teacher told me she would bring in a surprise the next day. I waited in eager anticipation. She brought large pieces of cardboard cut from a box, which we put on my desk so I didn't have to see the other children. One time I hid behind the cardboard in a corner of the room and listened to the teacher ask the other students where I was. I stayed there for quite a while.

It never occurred to me at that time to talk to my parents about the problem of bullying in school and the teachers never told them either. I accepted it as a fact of life.

> The single most important thing to learn from these social disasters is the importance of a social aide, who can be just as important, or more so, than an academic aide. Such a person could have helped me with the social challenges I faced in school, perhaps allowing me to devote more energy to academics during my early grades. Things would have been much better socially with such an aide. The social aide need not overtly appear as such, but knowing the aide is there would be reassuring to the child and also help keep order in the class when necessary.

In third grade the whole class went to a special room to do math. The math was difficult for me. I simply couldn't memorize the multiplication tables. Finally, I bought a multiplier pencil box for the wildly inflated price of one dollar from another student. Other kids asked me if I was crazy to buy it at such a high price. However, by using this device when I did multiplication and division problems, I eventually learned the tables, so it was well worth it. Perhaps this could be considered a piece of assistive technology!

The ability to understand other people's viewpoints took a long time to develop. One time around this period, my grandmother suggested that I give up my seat on the trolley to an older man who was standing. I remained seated, wondering why I should give him my seat. Although it makes perfect sense to me now, at that time it did not occur to me that an older person might not have the strength or balance to stand comfortably whereas I had more than enough resources to do so. My behavior was probably viewed as selfish and disrespectful by my grandmother and anyone else who had seen this incident, and I still feel embarrassed when I think about it.

Reading comprehension assignments in elementary school and beyond were always very difficult for me. I hated the "how well did you read?" section. I still have difficulties with reading comprehension as determined by a neuropsychological exam I took in November of 1996. I remember being infuriated at one of these assignments in fifth grade because it was entitled "How the Earth Was Formed." I *knew* how the earth was formed. Astronomy was my current special interest and I spent many hours reading astronomy books and copying their pictures and diagrams onto pieces of paper. The explanation in the reading assignment about the earth being the part of the back of a large turtle seemed so stupid that it infuriated me. Why should I spend time on such stupidity? Now that I am older, I can appreciate the story for what it is – an American Indian legend.

At times I feel that I am more literal than others. I remember being very upset about being introduced to the spelling concept of dropping the "e," if one exists, at the end of a word when one adds the suffix -ing. My concern over the letter was so great that I talked about it during a counseling session with a psychiatrist I was seeing at the time. He drew the letter of concern on a piece of paper and let it fall to the floor. I had to go rescue it. I truly felt bad for this letter that was cast aside and dropped to the floor. It was much easier for me at that time to imbue this inanimate object with feelings than people because humankind is full of unpredictable emotions that can be difficult to decode. It was as if the object had feelings of its own. Even now, when I see an object damaged I feel badly for it.

During the third grade I remember a classmate telling me that he felt like a pizza. I couldn't figure out what made him feel that way. Besides, he certainly didn't look like a pizza. Eventually I realized he meant that he felt like *eating* a pizza.

> When others tell a joke, I usually don't understand the punch line but pretend I do. Often I don't realize a joke is being made until the person talking specifically explains it to me. There must be some nonverbal cues that I fail to pick up.

As a child I often read books until they fell apart and then was sad when they disappeared. My parents must have thrown them out. A book about going to the hospital met this fate. I especially loved the Q & A section at the end of each chapter. There would be questions such as "How long until normal functioning can resume?" followed by the answer. The book *Dibs in Search of Self* by Virginia Axline (1961) was another book that met the read-until-it-fell-apart fate. I could identify with Dibs, who seemed so closed up but with the hard work of his therapist was able to open up and talk.

Catalogues and manuals were always of great interest and comfort as they were predictable. Often I compared different sizes and versions of products offered in the catalogues. Air conditioner capacities as expressed in British thermal units caught my fancy one day, so in every catalogue I would seek the highest capacity air conditioner that ran on 115 volts alternating current.

To their credit, my parents never hid from me the fact I was different from other children. The word "autism" was mentioned as if it were any other word. I feel that it is important for parents to disclose to their children their differences as soon as practical. While a child of six might not understand the complex terminology used to describe the autism spectrum, it is possible to talk about the set of strengths and weaknesses that everyone has. A good addition to such a discussion might be to explore how certain weaknesses are worked with or accommodated. For example, maybe Dad wears eyeglasses because without them he could not drive to work safely. Perhaps the child needs assistance with organization by carrying around a schedule book that is updated each day. Or maybe she needs to work out with the teacher (with parental assistance) a quiet place to go when she becomes overexcited (overstimulated).

Early disclosure of differences can avoid identity crises later in life when the challenges of being on the autism spectrum become more apparent and almost force the issue of disclosure. The other side of the coin is that finding out about one's autism spectrum diagnosis later in life engenders a great sense of relief and better self-awareness. This is because the person can now finally explain the struggles he or she has faced as a result of this disorder and can start working with the resultant set of traits, as opposed to against them. As knowledge of autism and Asperger Syndrome has become more widespread, it is becoming more common for parents to realize that their child on the autism spectrum often closely mirrors their own developmental patterns and that they too may be on or near the autism spectrum.

child awareness

apple far from the tree

We had an above-ground pool in our backyard of which I have fond memories. At first I was nervous to go in and struggled mightily against my father as he brought me into water that felt as cold as ice cubes. But after a while I grew to trust the pool and spent many an hour throwing water upwards with my hand and then hitting the drops of water when they came down. Watching the globules of water as they first ascended and then descended fascinated me. I felt like I was watching water move in slow motion. Splashing the water with my hand just before it landed in the pool felt really neat too.

Making bubbles with soapy water was another enjoyable activity. I was fascinated with individual soap bubbles as they represented an ever-changing world of color that was slowly overcome by browns and grays before they popped.

The intricacies of the inside of watches also fascinated me. Beginning at about age five, I would open the back of a watch and use a knife to unscrew all the little bolts that held it together and remove the gears. It was great fun to remove the catchment and allow the hands of the watch to spin freely, covering 36 hours in about 10 seconds. The second hand became invisible with the minute hand becoming nearly so. Sometimes I saved my money and purchased a wind-up alarm clock for $3.99 with the goal of extracting the balance wheel. Calling it a satellite, I would spin it for all it was worth.

> I have always wondered how I can have the fine-motor control to take apart a watch's gears while my drawing and penmanship when writing in script is so poor. Perhaps it is because the structure is inherent within the watch innards themselves, whereas when writing or drawing in freehand, I am forced to provide the structure. Even though I am well aware of my difficulties in penmanship and drawing, having to provide that structure from within myself makes it impossible for me to do these activities well.

> An accommodation for this fine-motor control issue for me is to use a computer. In many instances a computer can bridge the fine-motor issues between what I have envisioned and the manual graphical output. Like the watch, the computer frees me from having to devote energies to creating the structure and allows me to concentrate on the task at hand. In addition, computers are often particularly well suited for those on the autistic spectrum as they provide interactive consistency. A computer has the same response for a given input, so there is no body language or tone of voice messages that need to be decoded.

[handwritten marginal note: hand writing]

Following this, I developed a great love for electricity and electronics. As a result, I would scour the neighborhood trash and yard sales to pick up old radios and other electronic equipment, which I eventually took apart. A chemistry set from my parents gave me hours of pleasure.

Mechanics and spatial relations have always been a strong point of mine. From taking apart watches to radios and eventually bicycles and others items, I have always been curious about what makes things work. Towards the end of high school, I took a battery of tests to help determine potential college programs and careers that would be suited to my interests. The results that stand out most was the mechanical abilities test. I scored in the 99-plus percentile.

Ever since I was about five years old, I have been interested in visual phenomena. I noticed that distant objects would "follow me" as I moved about. For example, wherever the moon was in the sky, it remained in the same place wherever I went. If it was in the east, it stayed in the east. Objects that where a little closer did move to some extent. I noticed that two radio towers about a half mile from my home would seem to merge as one (actually one was behind the other) when it was time to turn onto the side street where my house was located. When I'd ask my grandfather about this, I never got a satisfactory answer. I believe, due to an inability to express myself clearly, he couldn't understand what I was talking about. I now realize that I was examining the phenomenon of "motion parallax."

Maps have always been an interest of mine. During my primary school days, entire walls of my bedroom were covered with maps of different countries, the moon and the solar system. I spent many hours looking at these maps and how the countries fit together.

When I was 12½, my mother received a call as part of a followup study by Dr. Janet Brown of the Putnam Children's Center. My mother reported I was doing well in sixth grade and had several absorbing interests. Although I was interested in and did well in science, difficulties in reading were still an issue as was socialization with my classmates. She prided herself on talking honestly and openly, which she still does, with her children.

By this time it had become clear that Martin would always need assistance in daily living. Robin, the only sibling not getting special attention, probably felt left out and very resentful. It is important for parents to spend time alone with the child without special needs because all children need a great deal of parental support, time and love.

CHAPTER SEVEN

Middle School

T hings got better in middle school and better yet in high school as I discovered the music room and spent a considerable amount of time there. I had finished about 10 years of psychotherapy to exorcise the demons that accompanied the autism. While the counseling didn't cure the autism, it did prove helpful for dealing with its effects on my psyche. Given that persons with autism or Asperger Syndrome have the capacity to come to terms with their own condition, talk therapy can be very effective in working with the secondary issues that may arise.

Most of my memories of these counseling sessions are of getting involved with objects. The tape recorder was a fascinating device that got much use during the sessions. For a few weeks I carried a globule of mercury around with me. This shiny, flexible, slippery metallic bubble was the greatest thing. I called it the "ig," and I remember the psychiatrist telling me that it wouldn't be a good idea to eat it.

I didn't like the play dough™ in the psychiatrist's office because it smelled and left a residue on my hands. To this day I still will not use play dough™ when working with children with autism or anyone else. However, there was plasticine. Although it still had a bad odor, it was tolerable. It was great fun to trap air bubbles within the plasticine and then pop it. A little while later, the psychiatrist showed me how to make flatulent sounds by clasping my hands together and moving them in a certain way. It was much fun then and I still can make the sounds.

The only representational play I remember was when I was about 9-10 years old. Using puppets to represent our family, I would enact various scenarios that closely related to the goings-on in our family. This was a period of great stress for my family. My brother, entering puberty, began to have grand mal seizures. His behavior could be a difficult challenge at times. As a result, there was much tension and yelling in our home. All of this came out in the representational play with the puppets. However, I didn't use them often because, like the play dough™, they had a disagreeable smell.

Martin's seizures were scary and could occur at any time. Often he would have a seizure in the middle of the night. Disoriented from the seizure, afterwards he might crawl underneath his bed or into my bed. I would then wake up my parents so they could put him back in his bed. Since we were sharing a bedroom, my way of dealing with this was to sleep with a crystal radio set I had built myself. I would plug the earphone into my ear and fall asleep in an attempt to block out the sound of a possible seizure later that night. It never worked. However, witnessing the seizure was never as bad as anticipating it.

As mentioned, I encountered fewer problems in middle school. The school being much bigger didn't cause any difficulty. However, one student managed to single me out and began making the familiar "I'm going to beat you up after school" threats. I promptly told my teacher. I don't know what the teacher said or did but the student never bothered me after that.

I am grateful to my parents for helping me see that teachers are real people. They did this by befriending them. One teacher came in and played the piano, another often visited us and became a regular part of our lives. He was my brother's middle school special needs teacher. As a result of this familiarity, I often wandered into the special needs classroom and got involved by helping with projects such as making soup to sell to teachers in the teacher's room. My desire to help in the special education room continued in high school as I played trombone for the students as a volunteer. After I graduated high school, my involvement in special education ceased and didn't resume until the study of autism became important to me in late 1996.

This special needs teacher was himself a special person. He organized weekend bicycle trips to Martha's Vineyard to "bring kids into the learning center" where he taught. I had always liked bicycles, but it was from him that my interest in bicycles took off in a serious manner. In eighth grade I went along on one of these two-day bicycle trips to Martha's Vineyard. After looking forward to the trip with much anticipation, a friend and I spent the entire two days exploring the island on our own. It never occurred to me that I should have informed our chaperone of our plans when we left early each morning for our rides. I only realized this a year later when my parents told me that the teacher had grown very concerned when he lost track of us for the entire day.

During our daylong explorations of the island, my friend and I discovered a steeply sloped beach with a crashing surf. Locking our bicycles, we scrambled down the beach to play in the water. The surf was wild and produced a strong undertow. The current was so strong that we were pulled under and dragged out to sea, even as we tried to anchor ourselves by digging our hands into the sand. The grains of sand stung as they were whipped along by the waves.

Although dragged under water and away from the beach with immense force, I realized that by relaxing and letting the water have its own will, I would pop to the surface in a few seconds about 25 feet from the shore. Riding the next wave in, I went through the procedure again. The next couple of hours were spent being battered by the god of water, Neptune. It was invigorating to feel pummeled by such a powerful force. Although it may have been dangerous, I had no fear and felt very aware, yet relaxed after I finished this aquatic sensory integration session.

Around this time I developed a fascination for locks. I would take them apart to see how they worked – it was a thrill to pick them open. On occasion I went to school early to see if I could pick any of the locks on the lockers. Sometimes I'd be successful. I never stole anything or even opened anyone's locker – the thrill of opening the lock was more than enough. However, sometimes I would move a lock to an adjacent locker, leaving the owner to wonder how his lock got moved.

When a group of children started to bully me, my math teacher, who was also an administrator, handled the situation in an interesting fashion. First, he brought me into his office and asked for a list of children who were giving me trouble. I was very nervous at his suggestion that we call each one down to his office in turn and confront them, but eventually he talked me into pursuing these confrontations.

With sweaty palms I waited as my math teacher-turned-protector called for one of the bullying students. Much to my relief, the student was absent that day. However, there were others who needed talking to. Soon the next classmate was located and was on his way to the office. Upon his arrival, the administrator explained that even though "Stephen might wear overalls to school or seem a little different," there was no need to "tease him." He made it clear that further teasing would not be tolerated. At the end of the 15-minute session, the administrator asked both of us to shake hands and my former tormentor returned to class. The confrontations worked. The students who were previously my enemies now talked to me in a reasonable fashion and at least seemed friendly.

Time was very important to me in middle school. Classes had to end on time. If they ended late it caused me great anxiety, as I knew I had to be at the next class on time. To me, the schedule dictated the timing of events and needed to be followed. One teacher called me his alarm clock because he could always tell by my actions when it was getting close to releasing the class for the day.

During this time I had regular appointments with a psychiatrist. His being only a few minutes late to a meeting was also distressing. He was able to calm my distress by promising to make up the time at the end of the current session or the following.

In my last year of middle school I discovered the music room in a round-about way. Based on an interest in electronics, I enrolled in an electronics shop-like course. I found the subject material fascinating. However, shop courses were often where the "tough" kids were, so it wasn't a place for me to accomplish anything. The teacher noticed my difficulties and arranged to have me transferred into band.

I went to band with my trumpet and have been playing in musical ensembles ever since. I loved the way the different-colored stage lights reflected off the shiny metal bell of the instrument. After a while I noticed the person next to me playing the trombone. I was fascinated by the larger bell and the piston-like slide. Around this time, a friend of mine announced that he was selling his unwanted trombone for $25.00. After blowing some notes into this instrument, I bought it. When I took it to a neighbor who used to play trombone, he responded with "Oh, my God!" and gave me my first lesson.

I loved playing the trombone! The pitch range was nice and, thinking back, it allowed me to work on some important abilities that often present a challenge to those on the autistic spectrum. The trombone worked well for me because I was able to practice muscle coordination, as the slide had to be placed in the correct position to play a note in tune. Since the positions of the trombone slide are on a continuum, there are no clicks or stops to indicate where the slide should go. The location of the slide has to be done via muscle memory with the ear checking for the intonation of the note.

Music for the Child with Autism

Music Enhances Communication

There are many benefits to using music with people on the autism spectrum. One of these benefits is that music provides the structural regularity that children with autism need. Within that structure it is possible to expand that child's repertoire of functioning.

Depending on the child's placement on the autism spectrum, I find that music assists with communication in different ways. For the child at the severe end, music is often *the* means of communication. Often, as I start a music session for children at this portion of the spectrum, the excitement and pleasure of music is clearly visible.

For the moderately involved child, music can serve as a carrier signal for verbal communication. One child, while having no functional communication, carried a storehouse of holiday and children's songs in her head. I only found this out one day when I didn't play the last note of a song. Not only did she say the correct word, she sang it at the right pitch. My only wish is that I would have been able to continue working with her in order to move this verbal ability towards functional communication. With limited verbal children of this nature, it is often possible to get them to vocalize and supply the missing words to a song they know by suddenly stopping the song and accompaniment at points of maximal tension. These places of "maximal tension"[9] (Miller & Eller-Miller, 1989, p. 65, 93) occur at the cadences during the last few notes before the final note of the music.

For the child with Asperger Syndrome or high-functioning autism, music can serve to organize the verbal communication

---

[9] The concept of maximal tension comes from Kurt Lewin's *A Dynamic Theory of Personality; Selected Papers*. Translated by Donald K. Adams. New York: McGraw Hill, 1935. This concept has been integrated in Miller's Cognitive-Development Systems Theory.

skills that already exist. All of my communications with one particular child with Asperger Syndrome are sung. If I mistakenly lapse into a typical conversational tone, he loses focus, engages in self-stimulatory activities, and drifts away. In addition, given sufficient interest on the child's part, the music sessions may transform into fairly typical music lessons.

During our first session I created a system where the child asked me for pieces of paper that had the letter names of the notes. Once the child had internalized this series of events, I expanded the routine by having him place the notes on the appropriate place on the music staff. This system was expanded further by having him draw a circle on the staff where the note belonged and write in the letter of the note. Then he would give the note to his mother. Fine-motor problems were present, and drawing a circle first helped confine where the note should go. Asking him on which space or line the note should go (as opposed to a generic "Where does the note go?") also helped. The system was expanded yet again by having the child guess which note I had in my hand. After guessing correctly, he had to write the note on the staff before receiving the piece of paper.

We then took turns, with him holding the notes and either his mother or I having to guess which note he had in his hand. When it came time for me to write the note on the staff, I would ask him in a singing voice on which line or space it went.

Other parts of the session were spent in imitative drumming, and later, work on the recorder. I made certain that we took turns in leading the imitation. This was a good activity to do when he seemed to be fading away and losing focus. His mother quickly caught on to our activities and participated very well in the session and we all had a pleasurable experience. The child has a lot of musical ability and using the Miller Method (1989, 2000), he was taught to play the recorder and later the piano, which he now plays well.

Music as a Means of Relating with People on the Autism Spectrum

Another important benefit from using music to work with people on the autism spectrum is that it provides a way of relating to others. The mother of the child discussed above felt that the music sessions were "able to take us away from the serious world of parenthood to the inner world of our son, where we could enjoy communicating with him without worrying about the rules of the outside world" (Jaklin Saikali, personal communication, January 30, 2001).

Sam, a 12-year-old child with Asperger Syndrome, is another child for whom music works well. At our first meeting, his mother expressed concerns about the challenges and difficulties Sam would begin to face as he entered adolescence, and wanted to prevent any behavioral ramifications. Sam had recently been rejected from a private school specializing in Asperger Syndrome for being "too low functioning." His mother, a professional musician, knew Sam had much musical talent but had yet to find anyone who could teach him how to read music. For all the children I work with, I request that a parent or significant caretaker join in the lesson for the following reasons.

  (a) It gives them another way to relate to their child.
  (b) They can work with the child in my absence.
  (c) Parents are the experts on their child.

Occasionally, the presence of the parent distracts the child from learning. In these cases I start by only working with the child and gradually involve the parent.

After several phone calls and e-mails with Sam's mother, she decided to hire me. In my first lesson with Sam I made gridlines on a notebook-sized piece of paper, resulting in a 7-row by 10-column box matrix.

After placing a few A's on the first line, B's on the second, down to G on the last line, I asked Sam if he would like to continue.

A	A								
	B		B						
C				C					
			D						
	F								
		G							

Eager to do so, he took the paper and started filling in the blank spaces with letters. Upon completion the piece of paper looked like this:

A	A	A	A	A	A	A	A	A	A
B	B	B	B	B	B	B	B	B	B
C	C	C	C	C	C	C	C	C	C
D	D	D	D	D	D	D	D	D	D
E	E	E	E	E	E	E	E	E	E
F	F	F	F	F	F	F	F	F	F
G	G	G	G	G	G	G	G	G	G

Like many people on the autism spectrum, Sam's need for order and task completion enabled him to accomplish a task of the lesson as well as work on fine-motor control and penmanship. Arranging his environment to take advantage of this characteristic worked much better than treating the need for order and completion as abhorrent behavior.

Later during the lesson, I started cutting the individual squares from the piece of paper and then passed the job over to an eager Sam. While he worked on this project, I drew a treble clef and staff on a larger piece of paper along with a lighter dashed line for middle C.

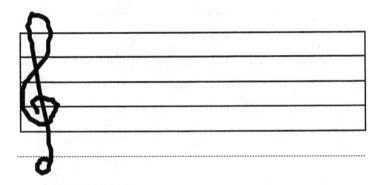

Then I drew a B on the middle line and asked Sam if he knew where C went. He responded with an anxiety-filled no! I drew the letter in the space above the B. A query about where D belonged elicited the same response. I now asked if Sam could just guess where the letter D might go. Now he answered correctly, and I had him write the letters in the correct places on the staff.

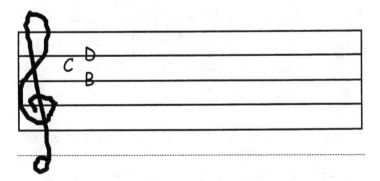

With the letter placements marked out, Sam was able to place the lettered squares he had previously cut out onto the staff in the appropriate locations upon my request. Soon we were spelling words such as "bag, dad, eat, and

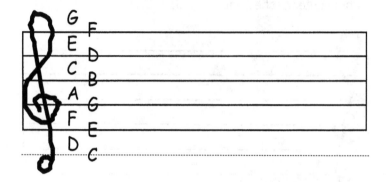

ace," followed by him singing simple songs such as "Twinkle, Twinkle Little Star" and "Mary Had a Little Lamb" as I played them on a musical recorder. Shortly thereafter we ran out of space on that sheet of paper, and it was time to make another sheet of staff paper. Sam's anxiety rose

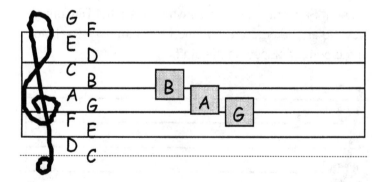

dramatically as I requested that he draw the staff lines and the treble clef this time. However, his reluctance melted away just as quickly when I offered him assistance in drawing the lines.

During the second lesson we progressed to writing the note letters on yellow stickies™ paper and posting them on both the staff paper and the piano keyboard. As Sam began to play "Hot Cross Buns," at first with the stickies™ bearing note names and then without, his mother was so overwhelmed with emotions that she broke down in tears. Being a musician herself, she knew that getting Sam to read music required a person who could meet him in the Castle, on his own terms, and give him the key to the door – and to decoding musical symbols. Sam looked over at her and with just a bit of nudging from me gave his mother a big hug. Who said that persons with Asperger Syndrome are emotionless?

It appeared that Sam was very anxious about failing at tasks. When he understood that he was in a safe environment without negative consequences for making mistakes, he did very well. I suspect that Sam's behavioral challenges in school were a result of not feeling safe academically. For example, during my first lesson with him, much of the conversation centered on his concern for what an F grade meant and that it was not good to get such a grade. Since the conversation did not interfere with our musical activities and, more significant, was important for Sam to process, there was no reason to stop the conversation.

The next time I saw Sam, there was no mention of grades. His anxiety about failing (at least in music) must have dropped considerably over the week. Sometimes Sam would immediately reject a request with "no!" only to commence the task a few seconds later. Perhaps his "no!" was in reality a bid for more processing time. Other than easily being overwhelmed with anxiety over failing, Sam seems to enjoy the continuing sessions and is a pleasure to work with.

By placing the notes on this staff in this manner, Sam learned how to read music and apply it to a piano keyboard. The difference between this approach and traditional music education is that the primary goal of decoding musical notation was incidental to the activity from Sam's point of view. In other words, a more traditional way to teach Sam music would involve spending a lot of time sitting in a chair explaining and showing Sam the names for the lines of the staff, notes, and their relationships. Instead, using a kinesthetic approach engaged and involved Sam in creating his own learning materials, which served to reinforce the physical activities of putting the notes in the right place on the staff, followed by placing them on the piano keyboard. For people on the autism spectrum, it seems important that the physical aspect of the body is in order before attending to the emotional and cognitive aspects. In addition, I was able to work on communication, taking turns, fine-motor control, and involving his mother in the lesson.

When time comes for Sam to get his first piano book, he will have a good background in the musical concepts presented in the text, having leaped over the initial learning curve involved in reading, understanding and converting notation to music on the piano keyboard. Not only does Sam benefit from social interaction and work on fine-motor control through learning music, he now has a skill that will enable him to successfully interact with others.

Music in Groups

When working with a group of children, music can be used to organize children's behavior by having them walk or otherwise move to the rhythm of the music. Often I will ask them to march in a circle as I play music on a keyboard. With help of aides, I have the students stop when I stop playing and continue when I resume. When the children understand when to stop and start, I turn this activity into a game similar to "musical chairs" where the person who stops moving last is "out" and will have to sit down. Realizing that it is unreasonable to expect these children to sit still with their hands folded while the game plays itself out, a shaker is handed to them – but not before they ask for it and identify the piece of fruit the shaker represents, if appropriate.

The worst thing, which I have encountered too often, is the sight of children sitting in a circle around a large instrument with nothing to do while they wait to take a turn on the instrument. Typically, when this is done, the children fall into a disorganized mass of stimming and challenging behaviors. This situation, caused by failing to engage all the children in a classroom, is entirely preventable.

Instruments and Ensembles

With the child who already plays an instrument, I introduce myself into his world by sharing the instrument via turn taking. When I play the instrument, the child accompanies me on percussion. Then we switch roles. The turns start out short and gradually lengthen to where I work on other issues such as verbal skills, writing, and motor control as needed. To establish equality between us, I must also take my turns doing anything I require of the student. I, too, for example, need to ask for permission to use the keyboard if the child is using it.

For the child at the high-functioning end of the autism spectrum, the school band may provide an important avenue for development. The trombone requires a good kinesthetic sense of where one's arm is in order to place the trombone slide in the right place for a note to be in tune. Other instruments, except for the stringed ones, require less ear-to-arm coordination as the pitches are obtained with the assistance of keys or valves. The French horn, however, demands much coordination of the embouchure.[10] Percussion may be another avenue. If complex rhythms present a challenge, the bass drum may be a good choice as the musical patterns are relatively simple. Additionally, the bass drum with its low and relatively simple sound waves is often easier for a person with sound sensitivities to handle. Finally, being at the rear of a potentially cacophonous musical ensemble may be of help as it is not as noisy there.

Location in the ensemble may have to take sensory sensitivities into account. If a student with autism insists on playing a certain instrument and it is clear that there will be problems with sound sensitivities, allowing the child to sit in a different location may be easier than rearranging the ensemble in a nonstandard manner. I skipped many jazz band rehearsals in high school because the director was unwilling to let me sit elsewhere than right in front of the blaring trumpets. In addition to the purely musical benefits, playing in an ensemble is good for working on concepts such as cooperation with others, coordination, and a sense of accomplishment.

Scientific Basis of the Benefits of Using Music

In addition to its educational value, music for children with autism has a physiological benefit. A research study by a neurologist at Beth Israel Hospital in Boston, who is also a musician, showed a physical change in the brain structure in people who started music training at an early age. It was found that a bundle of nerve fibers called the *corpus callosum*, which functions in carrying signals between the two brain hemispheres, is about 12 percent thicker among

---

[10] *Embouchure* is French, meaning flow into mouth. The word refers to the position and use of the lips, tongue, and teeth in playing a wind instrument. Sometimes it refers to the mouthpiece of a musical instrument.

keyboard players who started training before the age of seven compared to keyboard players trained later, or to nonmusicians (Schlaug, Jancke, Huang, Stagier, & Steinmetz, 1995).

While in middle school, I spent time with school guidance counselors. I never really noticed them until I got called out of a Spanish class one day to talk with one of them. I suspect that the stress from home emanating from my father having his first heart attack and losing his job affected my functioning in school. Perhaps one of my teachers had suggested to the guidance counselor that he spend some time with me. The guidance counselors had a bad reputation among the students as they were thought to be weird. However, knowing that they were counselors and having spent many years talking to psychiatrists, I looked forward to meeting him. I knew that the person who called me out of class wasn't "my" guidance counselor but he was neat enough to be with. We did imitations and I remember him doing an imitation of Hal, the wayward computer from *2001: A Space Odyssey*. The counselors were pretty cool people that one could just "be" with, and they were always willing to talk about feelings. For these reasons, I often asked the Spanish teacher if I could leave class and see the guidance counselor.

Two of the counselors held a class that seemed to be like group therapy. Here we talked about issues such as what defined being "tough." It was interesting to listen to the varied interpretations of "tough" beyond the usual attribution to excellence in sports and fighting skill in the school yard. I mostly listened and said very little unless I was asked a specific question. It was hard to talk about such things in a group. Even now it's easier for me to talk on a one-on-one basis. I find it even easier if someone asks me questions as opposed to having to initiate conversations by myself.

This class was where I first experienced embarrassment. I found that my face would feel flushed at the discussion of any topic I had a special interest in, such as when a teacher mentioned that she did yoga as a hobby. I felt that mention of my special interest would allow people to see all my thoughts and activities about it. Possibly I was afraid that if others knew I also practiced this activity, they would think of me as being stranger than I already was. This created a cycle of worrying whether this would happen followed by my struggling to keep it from happening. Around this time I remember reading that blushing was usually only noticeable to the person doing it. Reading this information reminded me of when in elementary school I heeded the lunch lady's advice that if I paid no attention to my enemies during recess, they would not notice my presence and I could subsequently enjoy the period. When I connected this information to blushing, blushing eventually became less and less of an issue also.

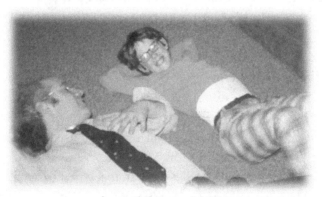

Around the age of 10.
Relaxing with a friend of the family.

In addition to spending time with the guidance counselors, I often made appointments to see the principal, whom I thought was a nice man. We talked about all kinds of things, including items I had noticed needing repair in the school. Objects in disrepair could be disturbing to me. It was as if the objects were not whole unless they were in good working order, especially when I had a good idea of how to fix them. The principal joked with me that as a result of my reporting services he would have to share his salary with me.

I have always found it easier to relate to people who are not of my age or culture. For example, during both elementary and middle school I got along much better with my sister's friends, who were about four years my senior, than with kids of my own age. These people were much more interesting to me and didn't have a need to bully. Certainly, I made friends with adults pretty easily too. This continued through junior and senior high school and in the workplace. This may be due to cultural expectations.

> People are finely attuned to the norms and behaviors of their own culture. Those who do not follow these norms, perhaps due to an inability to read them, are shunned on a conscious level at the public school age and on a more unconscious level as one goes on to college and the workplace. I can only recollect one incident of bullying at the college level, while more have occurred after graduation.
>
> In the workplace, I made friends with foreign people. I believe they accepted me more easily than Caucasian Americans because any subtle idiosyncratic behaviors I may have displayed were either not perceived or were attributed to being part of my culture. In addition, since people from other countries have their own challenges with cultural assimilation, they may be more tolerant of others' differences.

As the time for my Bar Mitzvah drew near, I couldn't grasp Hebrew to save my life. Finally, my parents audiotaped a cantor singing the "Bereshit," or the first three days at the beginning of the Torah, along with the other prayers in Hebrew. I had no idea what I was saying but I did a good imitation of the cantor right down to the dry gravelly voice, melodies and davening, which involves rocking back and forth from the waist up in a rhythmic manner as the Hebrew words are sung. Sanctioned rocking!

My mother, who is a traditional "Jewish Mother," told me that the reason why she and my father – neither of whom believes in organized religion – felt that my brother and I had to be Bar Mitzvahed, even though difficult, was that she never wanted to hear years later that I resented the omission of this rite of passage.

An Observation on High-Functioning Autism and Asperger Syndrome Parent-Child Relationships

As I come into contact with more and more people on the autism spectrum, I have noted a particular relationship that tends to form between the child (usually the son with AS) and one of his parents (usually the mother). I have also seen other combinations such as mother-daughter and father-son dyads. In a case illustrating a close mother-daughter dyad, the father, watching his wife and daughter sleeping in separate bedrooms, reportedly witnessed both daughter and mother turn over, awaken, open their eyes, and sit up in their respective beds simultaneously many more times than what would be expected by mere chance (personal communication, Eileen Torchio, November 1, 2002).

As a result of this close (some may even say pathological) relationship, it often appears that the parent becomes overprotective of the child with AS, making what may be perceived as too many accommodations. For example, I have heard many comments such as "If she would just leave him alone, let him make a few mistakes and grow up, he will be just fine." Given our society's norms for parental responsibilities, it is usually the mother who spends the most time with the children, so it should come as no particular surprise that it is the mother who spends the most time working with, accommodating for, and advocating for her child with autism. This closeness is compounded by the traits of high-functioning autism or Asperger Syndrome.

A person on the autism spectrum often has significant difficulties in perceiving nonverbal social cues in the environment. However, given enough intensive time with a loving and caring person, such as the mother, the person on the spectrum can become a master at reading these cues from that person. Combined with the tendency to fuse with another person's emotions (Miller & Eller-Miller, 1989), the individual on the spectrum often learns how to read this person's nonverbal cues so well that it almost appears that he is reading that person's mind. Due to difficulties in generalization, however, this ability to decode nonverbal cues does not easily transfer to other people. As a result, the mother becomes a sort of lifeline to the child as he learns to pick up social cues as translated through the mother. In other words, in the case of a mother-son dyad, for example, the child often looks to his mother's response to a social situation as a model for his own interactions.

Even after the child has "left the nest" and has become involved with a significant other, there is often an extended period of time before the person on the spectrum can transfer the ability to read nonverbal communication to that other person. For me, it took a good 10 years to accomplish this with my incredibly patient and understanding wife.

CHAPTER EIGHT

More Wonder Than Terror in High School

While middle school wasn't bad, high school was even better. My classmates spent less time being concerned with other people's differences. It seemed that students could move towards specializing in their own interests without fear. A friend of mine got heavily involved in photography while I spent more time in the music room. I felt comfortable with the older, classically trained teacher. I loved the structure of his music theory class, and he gave me lessons on the trombone during his free periods.

I made friends with many of the teachers. The guidance counselor was a particularly important man to me. I made weekly appointments with him and taught him how to play the flute or told him in excruciating detail which screw to turn in which direction to adjust the gears on his bicycle. But I couldn't seem to make my homeroom teacher like or even notice me. With his small goatee and tight mouth, he reminded me of a cat who was ready to pounce. One day I asked the counselor if I could switch to the homeroom of a teacher I liked better. An older man, this teacher taught United States history and wasn't liked well by other students as they thought he was boring. It is true that his classes were somewhat boring but he seemed like a nice person with a dry sense of humor. He also talked out of the side of his mouth, which I imitated for several years after graduating high school. After starting

*Age 15 on a bicycle trip in
Lenox, Massachusetts.*

college I continued to keep in touch with him. I enjoyed being with him and one day he even invited me to have lunch with him and his wife at his home.

Rather than automatically approving my request to transfer, the counselor suggested that I "find something like music to talk to him about." Following his advice, I brought in my flute, showed it to my homeroom teacher and played a few notes. This hard, seemingly unfeeling teacher turned into a warm and interesting human being. I took a class with him and would go to his home on occasion to fix his bicycles.

> Building a relationship with a person via an activity as the catalyst proved helpful. While this may hold true for most people, it is especially so for those on the autistic spectrum. Having an activity as the focus of the interaction reduces the reliance on being able to detect, accurately encode, and respond appropriately to nonverbal social cues.

At this time, English class and creative writing became a significant challenge. This was not surprising since I often had difficulty putting ideas on paper already in elementary school.

> In second grade, for a class assignment, I wrote a story about some kittens that alternated between existing as little

cats and puppies. In fact, they were in so much demand that they fetched $47,000 each; or the price of a house at the time. The ideas for this story were spun out of my current life events. Cats were a special interest at that time. One of my family's many cats had recently given birth to five kittens, we had acquired a puppy, and our house was on the market for the same price as these mythical felines sold for.

My teacher discounted the assignment as being babyish. However, if she had asked me where my ideas for the paper had come from, perhaps she would have been more understanding and helpful in getting me through the writing assignment. Catalogues and manuals were always much more satisfying as the meanings of the words were at the surface.

Creative writing, in particular, was difficult. By the time I got into high school, I seemed to be locked into getting a B minus on any English paper I turned in. While I liked to read, my comprehension was often a weak point. The interpretation and analysis involved in reading *King Lear* or *A Tale of Two Cities*, for example, was overwhelming. Beyond the incredibly long opening sentence in the latter book, about it being both a good and bad time, and

Age 15 with Martin.

the mention of a king having a large jaw, decoding the meaning behind or between the words was impossible.

The only time I got a better grade was when I wrote an essay about a student of whom my English teacher was fond. The topic given to us was about resurrection. Having had close contact with this person for several years, I knew she had many difficulties as a young child but was now in a much better situation. Writing about how she was a long time ago compared to the time when I wrote the paper netted a B plus.

Poetry was and still can be scary as it represents unknown meanings to me. I am unable to access the deeper meaning that *must* lurk underneath those words. At times words of poetry can evoke images of what seems like sensory input. However, converting these sensations to words is a demanding task. As with the exploration of feelings, perhaps it would help if I could find a trusted person with whom to analyze some poetry.

CHAPTER NINE

Heaven at Last
– in College

College was something I had been looking forward to ever since I spent a few days there with my sister when I was still in high school. People seemed friendly and were willing to talk with me even if they didn't know me. There was a good energy about the place.

At college I met people who appreciated me for who I was instead of making fun of what was different about me. During the last years of high school and throughout college I turned my interest in bicycles into employment at a bicycle shop. Running a small bicycle shop helped pay for school.

Once I had entered college, I never wanted to leave – still haven't – as I continue to study at one college while teaching at another. I like the predictable structure of the school day. At the undergraduate level I obtained two bachelor's degrees simultaneously, one in music education and another in accounting and information systems.

I drove my advisors and several administrative offices crazy as none of them could figure out what my educational plan was. I was the only one at my school to get these two degrees at the same time. My credits totaled the third highest number of anyone in the school, 224 credits to be exact.

College was an exciting time. I could be myself. There was none of the teasing and ostracizing by fellow classmates that had followed me throughout my school years. Students and staff were friendly and helpful. Also, there were enough people so that I could find others with interests similar to mine. Someone was always willing to ride a bicycle (even at midnight), play or listen to music. Courses were interesting too.

I found psychology courses to be particularly engaging because they helped explain how people behaved. When I became aware of the meaning of "body language" or nonverbal communication through a psychology class, I became fascinated with this mode of communication. This is probably because I have to analyze it pretty closely to understand this facet of interaction. In an educational psychology course, I did an extensive empirical study on nonverbal communication around the campus. For example, I studied what it meant if a person was sitting by himself at a table, sitting right in the middle, at the edge or towards the edge. To this day I enjoy reading books on nonverbal communication and find the studies on the human animal by Desmond Morris very fascinating. Of course, with his highly imitable English accent, Desmond Morris makes me want to watch his programs on educational TV even more.

Even in college, structure was still very important. I liked music theory and accounting because they both involved analyzing entities via their small parts. With music theory, a composition can be analyzed melodically for keys and for formal structure. Accounting can be used to analyze a business via its day-to-day financial transactions and financial statements. I mentioned this as I interviewed for an accounting job one time and got a standing ovation from the interviewer. I didn't get the job, however.

Structure in learning is necessary for me to do well in an academic setting. Otherwise I feel awash in an ever-changing sea of data. The structure can either emanate from the instructor or be self-imposed. Having an understandable and coherent structure allows me to create a framework in which I can be creative should the task require that. An information technology class I took as an undergraduate was highly structured. I took notes in a multilayered outline format using up to six different-colored pens. For example, the main idea was in black, subtopics in red, divisions of those in green and further prose-based explanations in light blue. The levels of indentation combined with the different colors helped me to map and retain key information for the class.

One place where the lack of imposed structure became a problem was when I started a research project for a physics of music class. Several other students and I found this teacher, while knowledgeable, quite boring. When allowed to select a topic of my liking, I chose to study the physics of brass instruments. However, not knowing what step to take next to complete this research assignment, I did not get much done beyond some initial research. Finally, the instructor got angry with me and I withdrew from the honors section of her class.

Later, during my doctoral program in special education, I took a qualitative research class where I found the structure difficult to grasp. I was aware that the qualitative research study paper had a particular format. However, the steps required to complete a qualitative research paper eluded me. Only after I spent several hours diagramming the process with geometric shapes and arrows did I gain a sense of where the different components of a qualitative study were placed and their relation to each other.

My first roommate in college was a friend from high school. This worked out well, because even though I settled in comfortably at school, it felt good to have a familiar person in an unfamiliar place. We got along reasonably well. Often when repairing bicycles, I would leave them in the dorm room that my friend and I shared. Upon relating this to my sister, she spent a long time telling me that it wasn't a good thing to do as my roommate might not like it. When my sister asked me if I would like it if my roommate had tripods and camera equipment strewn about the room, I answered that it wouldn't bother me. This discussion made me realize that just because I liked something, someone else could have a different opinion about it. As a result, my sister convinced me to move the bicycles out.

Dating

Dating is something I never quite understood and thankfully need no longer worry about since I am married. During my bicycle infatuation period, I was able to look at a bicycle for a second or two and record all of its data in my mind. I immediately knew the model, all the components, its gear ratios and often the weight in pounds. I would scour bicycle catalogues, books, magazines and stores endlessly. Often I would remark to others about the bicycles I had seen. When I commented to my parents about a bicycle as it passed by, they would often respond, "You need to look at *who* is on the bicycle, not the bicycle." I think they meant there was an attractive female on the bike and I was supposed to pay attention to her.

One thing that has always mystified me was crossing the border between knowing someone as an acquaintance or friend and being a couple. Even when asking trusted people about it, I could never get an understandable answer. As a result, I have had to let others cross the border to me rather than the other way around. I was often lonely and wanted to date but I could never figure out how to go about it.

During elementary and middle school I had a paper route. One of my customers had a friend who would hug me when we saw each other, and I still don't know whether she wanted to date me or was making fun of me. Since I didn't know, I did nothing.

A First Attempt

While I was in high school, my parents decided they liked a cute, female flautist in the school band where I played trombone. While my parents did not usually meddle in my affairs, they encouraged me to call and ask her for a date. I was nervous but went through with it. When I called, she said she was busy that day and that maybe we could get together later. I started talking to her in school. In response to my call to get together a second time, she said she was flattered but didn't want to go out with me. Upon my parents' urging I called back and asked why, to which she answered that she didn't think it would be a "good fit." I felt poorly that she did not want to date with me since it seemed that at least we had music in common. However, I did not have a crushing need to date her or anyone else at that time, so the encounter rapidly receded into the background. At other times when being with my parents at a restaurant or elsewhere, they would remark that a certain woman was "giving me the eye." But it was nothing I could detect.

One time I went "out on the town" with a bunch of coworkers from a bike shop in Cape Cod. We cruised down the main street over and over. It didn't make much sense to me. Finally, we went into a bar called the Velvet Hammer where the music sounded like the name of the place. I estimated the band was cranking about 700 watts of power. I couldn't hear a thing except for a wall of distorted sound from the guitar amplifiers. A woman named Robin sat across the table from me and I would like to have talked with her, but the overall noise level precluded any conversation. Also, I thought the lead singer, who looked like the manager at the bicycle shop where I worked, looked pretty stupid as he took a propeller beanie on and off while he sang, making me feel even more uncomfortable.

Ever since then, visiting bars has only served to remind me why I don't like to frequent them. Any activity where socialization is the primary goal has always been a complete bust for me. For those who are socially cue-challenged and have difficulty communicating in social situations, group activity where the activity is the goal may work. Finding a significant other is not something that can be forced and can only occur via increased circulation of a person through activities. Forced and contrived socialization doesn't work with me. Perhaps a support group and role playing about these things with others might have helped. However, I would have to be willing to go and talk about these things in order for it to work. And I wasn't.

Other than these two encounters, which cannot even be considered dating, there was no dating before college. Since I was working on two bachelor's degrees simultaneously, I kept myself busy taking courses all year, including the summer session.

Too Unaware to Know What Was Going On

Through a friend, one summer, I met a woman who started spending time with me. We'd hang out and she said she loved hugs and back rubs. The deep pressure felt good, so I went along with it. We would cook and go places together. Sometimes she asked if we could sleep together, to which I agreed. We didn't have sex and it seemed like an OK thing to do. Whatever she did to me, I would do back in almost an echopraxic dance. Echopraxia is the physical correlation to echolalia. Instead of repeating words like I did prior to the return of my speech, I imitated her movements. She hugged me; I hugged back. I received a back rub and then gave one in return. She was five years older than I was. On the phone she would talk so loudly that I had to place a cloth between the receiver and my ear to talk with her comfortably. In the course of our relationship she seemed to get frustrated. It felt like she wanted something but I was unable to comprehend what it was. One day she got very upset and started crying. She asked me what I wanted to do. This made me realize she wanted to be my girlfriend, which I wasn't interested in. I told her I wanted to be friends and left.

There was another woman whom I was friendly with in college. I would spend time with her and other friends along with her boyfriend. One time when greeting her she gave me what felt like a long, forceful kiss. I wondered if that meant she wanted something more but I didn't pursue it. This was the first time I really became aware of when someone might have wanted to be my girlfriend. Given my lack of awareness about the world of dating, I guess other women may have been interested in dating me over the years – much to my oblivion.

The First Real Girlfriend

Soon after that I was spending a lot of time with a female friend who lived down the hall from me in my dorm. The whole floor was for students in the honors program. By the end of that year, just about everyone had coupled up with someone else on that floor, leading to much room exchanging. As with the previous woman, we started spending a lot of time together, listening to music, talking and giving back rubs. She was my age and we had much in common, including a love for classical music and bicycles.

One night after listening to Beethoven's Ninth Symphony and bouncing on the bed and hugging each other in rhythm, she asked if she could sleep with me. I thought, "here we go again," but agreed. While I proceeded to sleep soundly all night, she told me that she had been awake all night watching me sleep. She didn't pressure me into sex and it seemed to be okay. She was my first real girlfriend. Being a couple seemed a cool thing.

It wasn't until our third year together that I was able to explore intimate relations with her in the fullest sense of the word. There seemed to be a wall that needed crossing, yet I was unable to figure out what that barrier was. Perhaps the problem was sensory overload. She must have had a lot of patience, gentleness and a willingness to accommodate differences even if she did not know what they were. During this third year she went off to Sweden to study, at which time we broke up.

Fear of Transitioning out of College

The second girlfriend relationship was born out of fears of having to transition out of college. The idea of leaving the paradise of university life was frightening to me. I had also heard that once one left the mating pool of undergraduate education, it was difficult to find a mate. Perhaps this relationship was an attempt to hold on to a piece of this time in my life. Unlike the first one, this woman was Jewish. We spent much time talking with each other but it wasn't a good match and the relationship only lasted for about six months. Although we shared a love for music, she preferred popular and rock whereas my interest remained in the classical realm. In addition, she insisted on sleeping with the radio on, which kept me up all night because I paid attention to the music rather than letting it remain in the background and lull me to sleep. Other differences that were important to me centered on lifestyle and career goals. She did not want me to become a teacher and that was too important to me to give up, so our relationship ended.

After graduating from college, I set my energies on locating employment, a place to live along with spending time with my family and friends. Occasionally I would feel lonely and wish there were a way to meet other people. I even considered using a dating service but had heard too many negative things about such organizations.

One time I even went to a bar with a couple of roommates, despite my earlier negative experiences. One of them had a lot of experience in the game of visiting bars whereas the other was about as inexperienced as I. I viewed this trip as a type of "lab" where I could study the art of attracting women with a willing and patient teacher. I knew he was good at attracting women because he "practiced" every weekend and more often than not brought a different female to our apartment.

We dressed up for a night on the town. After bar hopping between about five establishments, the data all seemed to be the same. My roommate had some sort of invisible skill that attracted women and made it easy for him to engage in conversations. He would point out a target, tell me he would "get" her, and then succeed in doing so. I, on the other hand, found the bars to be a basket of sensory violations – too noisy, too many people, too much cigarette smoke and too unpredictable. The other roommate and I would look at each other in amazement as our friend cruised from one woman to the next. I tried a couple of times to make contact but could barely hear what the woman said and couldn't think of any "small talk" to build a conversation.

An Encounter of a Third Kind

My next encounter with dating occurred about three years later while I was working as an accountant in a large bank and attending a Shiatsu school in the Boston area. Japanese for "finger pressure," Shiatsu is essentially acupuncture without the needles. As with the woman who talked too loudly into the phone during my undergraduate days, here too I failed to pick up on clues that could have led to intimate relations. I found out that a woman I had known in college about two years earlier had returned to Boston. A friend happened to mention her name and I got her phone number.

I first became acquainted with this woman by responding to an advertisement for free massages in the college newspaper while I was at the University of Massachusetts completing my undergraduate degrees. As a student of massage, she obtained plenty of practical experience through this publicity. The first four visits were free, with following treatments priced at eight dollars each. As one who craves deep pressure, I eagerly arranged for an appointment. For safety's sake, and to make sure this was an offer of legitimate massage, I brought a friend the first few times. Occasionally the woman's teacher would meet with us to check up on her progress as a massage therapist. These weekly sessions went on for about a year until I graduated and left the Amherst area.

Upon reconnecting we caught up with the goings-on in our lives over the past two years. When I brought up my interest in Shiatsu, she proposed that we exchange treatments once a week. Alternating between her house and my apartment, we exchanged treatments. Like the relationship two years earlier, these were non-sexual events. The only difference was that instead of only being on the receiving end, I was now able to provide treatment. After a while, we became friends. We would talk, walk around Harvard Square, climb trees, eat out, go to the theatre, or play musical duets. Since she was pianist, I also sometimes brought my trombone or flute to make music. Sometimes we played four-handed piano.

One day I noticed a pill bottle filled with Nardil on a shelf at the foot of her bed. Being familiar with the drug, I told her that my mother took this medication to treat her agoraphobia.[11] She informed me that she took the drug for clinical depression but never discussed it with anyone. She only told me because I already knew what that drug was prescribed for. I think her telling me this personal information meant that she trusted me.

> I often find people telling me very personal information. I think that is because I listen to them and accept what they say at face value without judgment. I accept people and situations for who and what they are. While many people

---

[11] Although Nardil is an antidepressant, Dr. David Sheehan, a psychiatrist, discovered the drug's ability to help alleviate the excess anxiety associated with agoraphobia in the mid 1970s. Dr. Sheehan is currently director of research of the College of Medicine at the University of South Florida in Tampa. Author of the book, *The Anxiety Disease* (New York: Bantam Books, 1986), he was formerly associated with the Harvard Medical School and the Massachusetts General Hospital.

appreciate this nonjudgmental approach, perhaps it sometimes prevents me from attempting to change negative situations into positive ones in a timely manner or even at all.

A lot of things to me just *are* – not good or bad – they just exist. In fact, I often wonder why others seem to exert a lot of energy deciding whether others are good, bad, ugly, or beautiful. This is a skill that I don't seem to have nor care to cultivate. This does not mean I am unaware of the difference between right and wrong or bad and good. I know that some historical figures were pretty evil and others did a lot of good, that some people are nice and kind rather than mean, and that there is an ethical way in which to lead one's life. It just seems to me that a lot of what goes on in the daily judging of others and their actions is not worth the energy expended in doing so.

This nonjudgmental approach once resulted in a misunderstanding with an online friend. She sent me a picture of herself, asking me how she looked. After responding through an instant message that I thought she "looked fine," I changed the subject. A few minutes later, she asked me if there was anything else I had to say about her looks, to which I again responded that she looked just fine. She asked me if there was anything wrong with her appearance. I answered back that every now and then I came across someone who was exceptionally beautiful or ugly but most people just looked OK to me, and that she was one of that majority of the people. Shortly thereafter, she got upset and logged off. A few days later she sent me an e-mail apologizing for getting upset and telling me that she realized I was her friend because we had things in common and that I valued her as a nice person rather than her visual appearance.

After a treatment one day my friend told me about a self-defense course she was taking called Model Mugging. She answered a few of the many questions I had about this program and then said, "some day I will show you how it works." One day after treatments she did her first demonstration. Suddenly enveloped by her from behind, I was very surprised. With my arms pinned to my side, I was immobilized. Not knowing what to do, I said "Bite!" as I thought back to the Model Mugging fighting techniques we had discussed earlier. She responded, "That's right. That is one thing you can do." Thinking nothing more about it, I took my knapsack and departed.

Graduation from the Model Mugging program entails using the techniques learned to fight off a rapist in a simulated situation. As it was customary for students of the program to invite their friends to this final exam, my friend asked me to attend. I went and was pleased to see her do well. In addition, seeing these women empowered to help themselves in such a dangerous situation was very moving.

The next week I received a letter from my friend that referred to both the Model Mugging final exam and to the day she had demonstrated what they learned in the self-defense course. She said I "shrank in size" after she enveloped me to which I said "Bite." She also wrote that she thought perhaps she loved me but would have to think about it for a while. At the bottom of the letter was a drawing of several instruments, including a trombone. My impression was that this was a very nice letter for her to write. I also knew that friends can love each other without having intimate relations, so pleased with this missive, I filed it away.

After a few more weekly massage sessions, she announced that she was feeling angry towards me and needed to talk about it. Not having any idea of what she wanted to say, I agreed to discuss whatever was on her mind to resolve the problem. She accused me of being sexually provocative with her and touching her genitals as I did my treatments. I was also accused of draining energy from her after she had gone through the simulated rape situation at the graduation from the Model Mugging program. Unaware of doing either, I apologized and promised to be more careful in the future. The next month went by without any similar incidents.

But prior to another treatment session she revealed that there was more she wanted to talk about and asked if I wanted to have the discussion before or after the massage. Choosing to air the issues before the session, I invited her to begin. As she sat down on my bed, she asked whether we should continue meeting. The subsequent river of pearl-like globes of water forming and rolling off her face was absolutely entrancing to me and I did nothing but watch. I had never seen so many tears at one time. After an hour of crying, going through an entire box of tissue paper and creating a soggy pillowcase, she said that she would have to consult her psychiatrist about whether to continue our friendship. After that I never heard from her again.

I often thought to call her since I was curious to find out what upset her so deeply, but I never did. I was sad that she felt unable to maintain contact with me. However, since what bothered her about our friendship was significant enough to discuss with a professional, I sensed it was better to leave things as they were.

Only after many years did I realize, perhaps for the first time, the contrast between my perception of how another person was feeling and what I thought the other person might be feeling. I now realize that the proper thing might have been to focus more on her feelings than on the more tangible river of tears that flowed from her eyes on the last night of our friendship.

Meeting My Future Wife

Dating ceased for the next two years until about half way through my master's degree in music education at Boston University. This time I started dating a Chinese woman two years my senior. I remember meeting her for the first time when she asked me to proofread some music for her. As she had only been in the United States for about eight months, her English was very difficult to understand. However, I still thought it was pretty cool that we could communicate enough for me to know she wanted me to look at her music. Eventually we took a class together and helped each other do homework. I would help her with the English and she would help me with the musical aspect of things. Gradually, we started doing more things together such as going to an Ethiopian wedding. One day I invited her to a music group meeting that my parents held twice monthly.

As in past dating experiences, she, too, was the initiator in crossing the borderline. I had no clue it was coming. Passing Plymouth on the way to that musicale at my parents', she asked if we could stop at a beach. I like the ocean so I agreed to stop at the first beach we saw. We found a beach near a restaurant and walked to the end of a long pier of rocks that jutted out into the ocean. At the end of the pier, while looking at the ocean, she suddenly made a small sound and hugged me. Not knowing why she hugged me, I hugged her back. Again, not being able to read the nonverbal cues, I defaulted to imitating her behavior. Finally she said that being Chinese, she couldn't act the way Americans do. Not knowing what she meant by that, I said "okay" and we held hands as we walked back to the car and drove to my parents' house.

About six months later we revisited that pier to examine our feelings of when we first came together. After a long embrace, lost in a world of our own with the ocean playing a musical theme, we heard a commotion coming from the shore. The patrons of the restaurant had noticed us and were giving us a standing ovation! We bowed deeply and quickly returned to our car.

We had known each other as classmates for about 18 months before we crossed the line between friendship and intimate friends in Plymouth. After an engagement of eight months we got married in 1990. She accepts my history with Asperger Syndrome and autism, but doesn't have an interest in pursuing it the way I do.

That is okay because I now realize that everyone doesn't have to be the same as I am. This is something I didn't realize when I had a relationship with my first girlfriend.

Being married to me must be an interesting and, at times, trying experience. Upon meeting, the fact that my wife-to-be's English was very poor did not bother me as I felt we could still understand each other. We were brought together via a common interest in music. I thought it was pretty neat that we could communicate with each other via music, another type of language, even though we understood little

On the beach with my wife, Yi Liu.

about each other's spoken language. There was much to relate to regarding music, classes, classmates, professors and other happenings within the music department, and this served as a common ground for our relationship to grow.

Before our marriage, on several occasions, my mother and I would explain my past experience with autism to Yi Liu. Using words, imitations and pictures I believe she got an idea that something had happened in the past but wasn't sure of what it was we were trying to communicate. Finally, she termed what I had as "closing disease," which wasn't a bad interpretation given the language and cultural barriers we faced in explaining my history. I later found out that the literal Chinese translation for autism in indeed "self-close." At that time the study of autism was not important to me and was something I considered a thing of the past. If it had been as important to me as it is today, I would have found a

Chinese doctor who knew what autism is and asked him to translate what my mother and I were trying to convey.

About six years into our marriage, my interest in Asperger Syndrome and autism had grown significantly. Upon researching the Internet on this subject, I discovered a Chinese translation of an autism Internet web page.[12] When I showed it to Yi Liu, she immediately understood what I had been trying to explain to her for the past six or seven years. She told me that in China, children with autism who could not make it in public school remained at home with their parents and out of sight of society.

She marveled at what my parents had done for me and thought the whole thing was very interesting. Her sense of wonder continued until I presented the remaining pages of the translated web site to her. After reading the translation of the *Diagnostic and Statistical Manual of Mental Disorders* of the American Psychiatric Association criteria along with the social, employment and learning challenges faced by people with Asperger Syndrome and autism, she was horrified. Or rather, Yi Liu was not directly frightened by the information but by the idea of others finding out.

> According to an old Chinese belief, a child is born with a disability as a result of a prior misdeed by the parents. While this is no longer generally believed by people of the Far East, as in many other cultures the shame in being associated with someone with a disability remains. Until recently, children who were different and could not be accommodated by the regular school system were kept at home and hidden from the view of others. Fortunately, great strides have been made towards providing help to children with autism via the newly founded Beijing Institute of Autism.

---

[12] An overview of autism has been translated into several languages at <http://www.autism.org.>

Regrettably, my wife remained very fearful of others knowing about my history with autism, which often caused friction in our relationship. Sometimes I feel this reaction may be a result of her growing up during the police state of the Cultural Revolution where no one was to be trusted, especially with private information. My wife's reactions seemed to parallel those of a parent who has just received a diagnosis of autism for his child. After going through the stages of shock, denial and anger, there seems to be an acceptance and appreciation for what people who are wired differently can bring into their lives. As time goes on, Yi Liu has become more comfortable with my involvement with the autism spectrum. She recognizes that this is something I have success with, enjoy doing and where I can be of assistance to others. I have her full support for my endeavors in this area.

After Yi Liu became able to properly define autism and Asperger Syndrome, she told me that during the early stages of our relationship she noticed something was "different" but was unable to put her finger on it. Yi Liu's observations of people are often accurate and I find it interesting that she did notice a "difference."

She also has great powers of facial recognition. I continue to stand in wonder as Yi Liu looks at a family picture and is able to draw out the relationships between the people both within the photograph and any relatives who happen to be standing in the room at the same time. Her ability to follow plot lines in movies is also excellent.

As Yi Liu's interest in this book grew, she came to a point where she wanted to make her contribution. Below are a few words from my wife about how she sees me.

About My Husband

We have been married for 10 years until now. I still remember the day we became boyfriend and girlfriend. I still remember that day, that moment: March 8, 1989. The day was cold; the heart feels warm. I used to have a roommate. Even before we came together she and I saw "xin li jang lie." This Chinese word translates to having a psychological difference. And he has a lot of interest in things that for me are very difficult to understand.

I have noticed some unusual habits. He has a sensitive ear. I am a musician and have a very good ear but my husband seems to have a different kind of ear sensitivity. He can hear much higher pitches than I can. For example, for a long time I would often find a wind-up clock missing. When I asked my husband about it, he told me that he put it under a chair or couch cushion because he could not stand the constant ticking noise. This is difficult for me to understand because this small ticking sound does not bother me at all. In fact, I like it. Whenever I watch TV, my husband tells me it is too loud. He always wants to turn the volume so low that I almost cannot hear it. He is very good at imitation. He pronounces the Chinese language with all its tones very well. Many of my Chinese friends say his pronunciation is excellent. Sometimes they are fooled until they exceed his limited vocabulary. All of his Chinese was learned from me, my friends and from auditing a Chinese language class for one semester.

I didn't know my husband had a diagnosis of autism until about three years ago when he began to get very interested in this subject. I figured out he sees a lot of things normal people can't see. He seems to care about and hear very small things that others do not perceive. For example, he seems to be able to judge what kind of person someone is. One time, during a visit to my friend's house, my husband told me he heard a baby. I didn't realize there was a small child in the house. When I asked my friend about it, I found out that her parents were taking care of a friend's baby while the parents worked during the day.

He likes to watch boys' scientific and weird space movies. Whenever I try to watch TV with him, he always falls asleep. Also he has a lot of interest in stores such as Brookstone and Sharper Image that sell strange devices for squeezing and pummeling. He has a lot of strange toys such as a large tarantula spider encased in clear plastic. He also brings home a lot of strange stones. He seems to see something in them that I cannot see. One day, when trying to practice a dance, he spun around with me so fast I almost threw up. But he kept saying "faster, faster." He was fine after spinning around but it took me almost an hour to recover from my dizziness.

His body is very sensitive. No tickling, especially the feet, is tolerated. He likes it when I hold him tightly. He sees things in print that I cannot see. One day he showed me the words around the portrait of President Jackson in the new $20 bill we used to pay for our meal in a restaurant. I insisted that this area was merely a design while my husband maintained that the "design" was actually words stating "The United States of America." It was only after much studying of the banknote that I could see it too. But I never would have seen it had he not pointed it out. The next day I went to prove it by letting one of the children with autism at a school where I teach see if he could read the words. He looked and read them off easily.

*I was so surprised at my husband's fascination with air-
planes. He loves to look out the window at the ground as
the plane flies. Myself, I'd rather stay on the ground where
I can still get up in one piece if there is ever a problem.*

Movies and TV

Movies and watching television have never been a strong point
for me. During my elementary school days, whenever I was at a
friend's home and he wanted to watch television, I would go home.
I thought that if I wanted to watch TV, I could do so at home, but
I rarely watched it at home either. I remember when my parents
put a TV in my room and made a big deal about it. Some of my
friends talked about having a TV in their room and getting into
trouble with their parents because they watched it too much. I
still rarely watch TV except for the news and documentaries.
Often I fall asleep when the TV is on. Situation comedies and
other shows about people never interested me. Until I reached my
mid twenties, I thought the term "sit-com" meant that this type of
comedy was to be watched sitting down in a chair or on a couch.

Some exceptions include "All in the Family" and "Lost in Space."
While I don't go out of my way to watch "All in the Family," I will
watch it if I notice it is being broadcast. I am able to keep track of
the relatively few characters on the show because the location and
appearance of the characters remain mostly the same. The outlandish things that Archie Bunker says and his warping of the
English language are also humorous. I enjoyed "Lost in Space"
during my elementary school years for similar reasons. Few characters were involved, and when the occasional guest character
appeared, it was usually just one, which I could keep track of.
Eventually I got bored with the show because it seemed preposter-
ous that when they landed on a planet, they were always able to go
out and breathe the air without needing a space suit or other air
supplies. Had I known about "Star Trek" at that time, I probably
would have watched that show.

The same reaction extends to movies. Often, movies and television are a visual-aural bath for me where I have trouble tracking everything going on. I continue to be astounded by my wife as she keeps track of what the characters are doing and who they are, whereas I focus on more mechanical, aural and special effects-related aspects. I enjoyed the recent version of the movie "Titanic" for this reason. My wife and I sat four rows from the front of the screen. The flyovers of the boat and scenes of water pouring in were great to watch from this distance. There was no visual over-stimulation as I had initially feared when we took our seats because the movie was very slow moving in a visual sense.

CHAPTER TEN

The World of Work: From More Conformity to Less

Where Do I Fit In?

After receiving my bachelor's degree in music education and accounting and information systems, I set forth to work in a medium-sized certified public accountants firm. Boy, was that a mistake. And as a result, I was let go after only three months.

I spent hour after hour preparing financial statements by hand for the auditing of mutual funds, so much so that I got tendonitis in my wrist. As the low man on the totem pole, I would spend a lot of time verifying the work others had done. Even though I had just graduated as an honors student with a bachelor's degree in the field, I often felt my coworkers were speaking in another language when they explained procedures and told me where different documents were located. It seemed as if I had been dropped into a foreign culture. I felt as though I needed to be shown step by step in a discrete manner to get a grasp of what was expected of me, but no one was willing to do that.

I was closely supervised and was expected to fit in with all the accountant/business employees. The business uniform was a suit and tie, which drove me nuts. I can't stand to wear a tie. The only way I could survive was to ride my bicycle from where I lived (about 7 miles) to work and enjoy the out-of-doors for an hour and a half each day. It took 45 minutes to get to work this way as opposed to two hours by public transportation. Made sense to me.

Riding my bicycle to work and changing into my suit in the basement of the office was too weird for them. The personnel officer told me that I had better take public transportation and arrive at the office in my suit. Thinking back to that time, I realize that I could not possibly have chosen a place that was more conservative and conformist. After a while I spent most of my time in their library reading business reference material as the supply of work seemed to dry up. On occasion, I would seek out work from coworkers or drop into one of the senior managers' office for a chat.

An assignment with a fellow accountant at the firm didn't work out well. I never understood what he wanted and he seemed irritated by the things I did. For example, the bank where we worked was overheated. In response to that, I often opened the window and took off my shoes when I was sitting at my desk out of view of other people. He didn't like that at all. While auditing a ledger I made a comment to this colleague about my difficulty in reading some of the numbers the client had written that came back to haunt me shortly thereafter.

One day the personnel officer called me into his office and told me he was letting me go. I just didn't seem to fit, he said, and suggested that I might have a disability that I had failed to disclose when I interviewed for the job. That disability may very well have been there. However, to me, it was something of the past and it never occurred to me that any accommodation may have been needed. I just blamed myself, thinking I was stupid because I didn't "get it." Getting fired was very humiliating and embarrassing to me. With a fuzzy, heavy feeling in my head I gathered my belongings and left. I felt more confused than anything else, because I couldn't understand what I had done that caused my employer to act in this manner. Perhaps a bit more patience and a willingness to work with me on getting acclimated to my position would have netted them a hard-working, focused accountant.

Working at the accounting firm had been a mismatch from the beginning. I was introduced to the firm by a consultant who interviewed prospective accountants for several small and medium-sized accounting firms in the Boston area. When I interviewed, I was asked questions about research to which I answered that it was something I enjoyed. The interview concluded with the consultant saying that I was off to a great start and should be hearing from interested firms within a couple of days.

A few days later I got calls to interview at three accounting firms. Offers were extended from all of them, and I chose the one that worked with mutual funds. Mutual funds were a special interest of mine at that time and the idea of auditing a mutual fund by myself within a few months was attractive. But it soon became apparent that this company was not the place for me.

When I informed the consultant about losing this job, he told me two interesting things. First, he wondered why I chose that particular firm as it was the most conservative of the three where I had interviewed. Second, he revealed that he had told them that while I would be a good worker, they might have to tell me "not to wear my army boots in the office." I'm not sure what that meant, except that perhaps he was suggesting that they are fussy about the appropriate behavior and demeanor of an accountant, and therefore needed to provide me some guidance in this area.

My next job was at a large bank as a portfolio accountant. I made trades, received interest and dividends, and created regular financial reports for $750,000,000 of pension fund money. I had now learned better how to blend into the business world. But while they tolerated my riding my bicycle to work, I was miserable in the business culture; additionally, the assumption that I had left the bullies behind in middle school was incorrect. They were here too. Except for friends from India and Ethiopia, I kept to myself. I was not interested in spending the day yacking about team sports and how much a certain couch cost. I left this job after 15 months to teach business at the vocational and college level.

> The strange thing is that I find the STUDY of business, taxes, the stock market, and so on, fascinating. I also enjoy TEACHING business subjects, but not as much as teaching music. I simply can't tolerate working with the personality profile attracted to this field.

Teaching was for me. My first teaching job was at the American Business Institute. While a tie remained part of the dress code, the atmosphere was more relaxed than at the bank and there was nobody watching my every move. My supervisors and the students were closer to accepting me as myself than in any previous position. They actually respected that I rode my bicycle to work. That job ended after two and a half years when the company went out of business. My next place of employment was at Katharine Gibbs, a finishing school for secretaries. When taking that position, a warning like that issued by the robot on the TV show "Lost in Space" should have gone off in my head. Too strict a dress code. I was let go from that place after two years. This job was followed by two years of part-time teaching positions in various colleges in the Boston area.

When I got my job as professor of music and computers in January 1994, I knew I had found my niche. I could do what I loved and expend much less energy trying to blend in. As long as the students were happy and learning what they were supposed to, the administration did not get too involved with my activities there.

Several people at this college respected what I did for the school and served as my mentors, informing me of potential political blunders I might be about to make and being ready to help bail me out if I got into trouble. It is often difficult for me to read the political wind of things, and I'm terribly susceptible to bully types who cross my path.

Those of us in the Fine and Performing Arts are frequently expected to be somewhat quirky and that suits me fine! By the way, I didn't have to wear a tie at this job! Some people at work may have sensed that I'm different but I don't think that the general school community had a true sense of who I am.

After this trip through various places of employment, certain things became clear to me. To survive as a full-time employee of an organization, I must follow these tenets.

1. I must know myself well enough to know where in the workplace I fit. I seriously misjudged that relationship as I entered the business world. The conformity along with the suit-&-tie thing doesn't work for me.
2. Close supervision of my day-to-day activities doesn't work for me. I do much better if I'm given a task and a period of time in which to accomplish it, usually in a way that it hasn't been done before.
3. I must find a mentor or mentors I can trust.
4. Having an interest in a particular field doesn't mean that it is good for me to work in it.
5. There is more to life than work. Really? Yup! I'm still learning that.

However, my work at the college was circumvented by a politically oriented challenge that I was unable to handle. As a new full-time faculty member, I had the full backing and support of my dean in teaching my classes along with course and curriculum development. Upon her direction, and with the approval of the chair of my department, I set out to restructure the music degree offerings and add new courses to the curriculum. Whereas at the time it was only possible to declare a general major of music, my idea was to create different options within that degree. My sense that students would more readily identify with a specific program rather than a general music degree was verified as the number of declared music majors doubled soon after the change was implemented.

After following the bureaucratic maze of policies and procedures along with much collaboration with other faculty and staff, the restructured program was approved by a vote at an all-college forum. However, within this victory for my department and the others involved were sown the seeds of destruction for my continuing as a professor at this school.

A long-term faculty member felt slighted by my failure to consult with him during the restructuring plans. He taught a single music class, had been in the college for almost two decades, and was very influential in determining academic policies within the institution. As I was new to the college, it never occurred to me to consult with this colleague because he was the chair of another, seemingly unrelated department. I therefore didn't realize the error as I continued to reconfigure the music program.

While I did confer with other members of the music department as I plodded through these modifications, I now realize that I should have expanded my inquiry to include additional people who were working within the music department. Perhaps my overreliance on the documented organization chart rather than the informal organization led to my overlooking this person.

My failure to sense this situation, combined with the challenges of not being able to read subtle social situations (office politics), resulted in this person's initial displeasure with my working at the college. Unaware of the gravity of the situation in this person's mind, I never took steps to make amends for my perceived transgressions towards him. From that point on, he was always at the ready to oppose further plans for developing my department.

For the first three years at this school I enjoyed a well-established support system that encompassed colleagues as well as the administration, ranging from the dean all the way up to the president of the college. Thus, despite the attempts of the faculty member I had offended, along with a cadre of individuals who supported his wish to have me dismissed from the position of music professor, the administration saw that I was continuing to make a substantial contribution to the college and kept me on. Some of these contributions included doubling the number of declared music majors and acquiring almost $40,000 of musical equipment to the school via grant proposals.

Unfortunately, over these three years, the support base I had established with the administration and other faculty eroded as many of them left the college for various reasons. As soon as I was without this support, the offended faculty member was able to get the school to conduct nationwide searches for the music position I had held for three years. In the first search, I was one of the top three candidates for the position. Another person was chosen but declined the position. The second time, I received the greatest number of votes from the search committee. Yet, despite the search committee's recommendation, along with the agreement from the dean of the department, the music position was suddenly and strangely terminated.

Emotional Aftermath

Losing this job has been very painful to me. For a time I had thought I had a good chance at employment for life at a job I enjoyed. The position seemed like a dream. I could do what I loved and there was time to pursue my interests in other areas such as autism and Asperger Syndrome and bicycles. Losing the job, despite following all the procedures I thought necessary to retain my position, was a serious blow.

As this drawn-out process continued, I realized that I needed to do something to sublimate the energy created by the angst of the looming possibility of becoming unemployed. A majority of this energy was devoted to gathering information about and developing contacts in my future field of work: the autism spectrum.

I was very angry. It seemed so unfair. With much trepidation I filed legal action with governmental agencies and with the teachers union. I was reluctant to request assistance from the teachers union as confrontation is difficult for me. I suspect this is because it involves strong, unpredictable emotional behaviors and reactions. For a person who likes things to be scripted before they happen, the unknowns of confrontation can be very frightening.

Even though I was still working, I experienced a big change in my attitude towards my place of employment. Until this time, aside from my wife and family, I had given this position first priority in terms of time and energy. Because I received such positive feedback from the president of the school and other superiors, I felt what I did there was worthwhile and appreciated.

After realizing that the school – or specifically, a few key people – did not concur with this view, I redirected my energies elsewhere. It no longer seemed necessary to be friendly with most of the people there, and certainly not perform any job functions that were beyond what was described in the teacher's contract. Unfortunately, it was these additional things beyond the bare teaching and advising of students that had given me a lot of satisfaction.

As a result, the position became a mere shell of its former self. I did as I had seen many other teachers do: arrive, teach, help the students (some colleagues didn't even do that), and leave. It was very difficult for me to change my work habits to this minimalist approach, as it was my nature to continually work towards making the school a better place for the students.

Whereas this position had been a source of enthusiasm and energy for me, it now was an emotional drain. Suddenly I realized why others at this institution seemed to put in a minimal effort. Perhaps they, too, had been burned by office politics and felt unappreciated.

Dealing with Emotions

There are times when I find myself very interested in the study of feelings and emotions. This happens especially when I see someone experience a strong emotion or I sense that I don't seem to have an "appropriate" emotion for a given situation. Either I think about these emotions myself or I talk about them with trusted people. I find that music can serve as an amplifier of feelings. If I am in a particular mood I listen to, or run in my head, music expressing that feeling. Sometimes I sense that feelings are something that can be taken out of their box, examined, and put away when you are done with them. Sometimes I think that I should be feeling a particular emotion but it just doesn't seem to be "there" to feel.

> After my first girlfriend left to study in Sweden for a year, I played Gustav Mahler's Ninth Symphony. The last movement, in particular, helped me deal with the sadness and loss relating to her departure. Added to that was the realization that our relationship as boyfriend and girlfriend was probably over.

The Power of the Uttered Word

I have always been mystified by people's ability to extract strong emotional meanings from words. The deep feelings brought on by poetry or music had always escaped me. In fact, until I was about 20 years old, I didn't like to listen to choral music or even most symphonic works with vocal parts. People would describe to me how "deep" or moving certain lyrics were. However, no matter how carefully or intently I would listen to these lyrics, the emotional stirring they were supposed to produce continued to elude me. Knowing that songs could be very moving to people, I often wondered what was wrong with me as I was unable to decode these strong emotions from text that was put to music.

It wasn't until about the age of 35 that, through text put to music, I learned the potential emotional impact of words. This occurred as I was teaching a course in music appreciation. After listening to "A Survivor From Warsaw"[13] by Arnold Schoenberg, I was suddenly overcome by emotion and was not able to speak for a couple of minutes afterwards. My students asked me if I was okay. All I could say was that this was a very moving piece that deserved a few moments of silence when it was finished.

After this breakthrough, I was able to explore moving feelings from other songs such as "She's Leaving Home" by the Beatles and "Der Erlkönig" by Franz Schubert. I had known these compositions for some time but they seemed like new pieces to me now that I was able to decode their emotional content.

Perhaps my interest in studying feelings and emotions stems from the fact that they don't come "naturally" to me. The study of nonverbal communication helps me build a lexicon to assist in decoding its meanings. Emotions and feelings get examined and analyzed in a similar way.

Decoding facial expressions of others is difficult. On occasion I display either an inappropriate facial expression or emotion or perhaps none at all. Several times I have been asked if I am feeling a certain way and the question comes as a surprise because, in fact, that is how I am feeling. For example, people sometimes ask me if I "am alright" or if "everything is OK." I wonder if this is due to a disconnect between how I actually feel from what my body is displaying at that time, or whether my body is accurately showing an emotion with which I am out of touch.

During my undergraduate days I underwent a few counseling sessions to work through some issues of family relations. Several times the social worker asked me how I felt

---

[13] Written in 1947 by Arnold Schoenberg for narrator, chorus and orchestra, this piece is about the Jews' plight and suffering in the Nazi concentration camps. Making use of English, German and Hebrew, this composition is very moving while at the same time utterly terrifying.

about what she was talking about because she said she could not tell by reading my face.

When working at the large bank discussed earlier, I received a phone call one day that my parents had been involved in a car accident. Following the call I told my coworker that I would ask my supervisor for permission to leave early to see my parents. My coworker said, "You go; but don't laugh when you tell him." Apparently, even though I felt fearful about my parents' conditions, an inappropriate smile or laugh must have escaped that caught my coworker's attention.

As I sometimes have difficulty matching the meaning of my own verbal channel to that of the nonverbal pipeline, decoding the two simultaneously also presents a significant challenge.

When dealing with emotionally charged issues, I often sense that there is something important to be worked out; however, I feel an overwhelming conflict. Perhaps this is because emotions are a sort of "second" language to me. Not only do I have to decode the words on the verbal channel, I also have to deal with the nonverbal channel consisting of body language, facial expressions and tone of voice. To further confuse things, what is actually being said may be different from what is implied by vocal inflections and other components of the nonverbal channel. In other words, having to "read between the lines" confuses things.

When this happens, I know that something is going on but I'm not sure what it is. I want to do something about it, but not only am I unsure of what to do, I don't know how to do it. As a result, too much energy goes into processing the situation and a shutdown occurs in the communication arena. I become unable to speak. Telling me to talk does not help in these situations.

With emotionally charged situations I often feel like I am in a foreign land where I know just enough of the language to get an idea of what is happening, but no more. This is similar to being at a party with my wife where everyone is Chinese. I know enough Mandarin for rudimentary communication of pleasantries and to have a general idea of the conversational matter. The difference is that there is no feeling of discomfort because my limited comprehension is expected as English is my primary language. In addition, knowing that my wife is available to decode communications as needed is very helpful.

When dealing with emotionally charged situations with other people, I find it helpful if others can say exactly what they mean along with creating a feeling of safety and trust. If this happens, I feel freed from the concern of having to create an appropriate response. Some phrases that I keep in my response repertoire for these situations include "What can I do to make you feel better about this?" or "Look, I sense that you have some strong feelings about _____. Can we talk about it?" While having an algorithm or method for handling these types of situations helps, it does not approach the facility others off the autism spectrum seem to have for these emotionally charged situations.

CHAPTER ELEVEN

Back to School: Master's and Doctorate Degrees

D uring my time at the American Business Institute, I began to search for a graduate school where I could study for a master's degree in business. Because I was teaching business, it made perfect sense to get a degree in that field. Knowing that I would never return to a corporate environment, I had decided to make teaching a permanent career. So, after receiving information from several schools, I made an appointment at the Graduate School of Management of a major university in my area. I talked with them for about a half an hour, got my information and left.

On my way home, I stopped in front of the School for the Arts where the music department resides. Telling myself that I wouldn't get a master's degree in music, I nevertheless decided to go in and ask a few questions about the program. At this point I was torn between getting a master's in a subject that I knew would lead to higher-paying employment versus a subject that I knew I would enjoy. Since I was teaching business-oriented courses, the rational, cognitive side told me to get a degree in business whereas the emotional side led me into the Department of Music. Four and a half hours later I emerged from the building convinced that my master's would not be in business, but in music.

The master's program in music education was very enjoyable and a good educational experience. The courses in music education, theory, history, research, and lessons on my trombone went well. I liked researching in the library; made friends; the professors respected my work and I did well overall. Theory classes were my favorite as I liked how the analysis of music revealed its structure. Composition being a strong point, I took several classes in this area and wrote a brass quintet as my master's terminal project.

As mentioned earlier, it was during this master's degree that I met and married my wife, Yi Liu. Things were going well. I taught computer and business classes while also attending to my academics. Since I was studying music, I felt that I should start getting experience teaching in this field. I even convinced the dean at the Katharine Gibbs school where I was working at that time to let me teach a course in music appreciation.

I enjoyed the master's program so much that I was content to continue taking classes and delay graduation indefinitely. However, upon hearing my plan of doing so, my music advisor suggested that I quickly graduate and apply the courses I was interested in taking to a doctoral degree. Following her advice, immediately upon fulfilling the requirements for the master's I entered the doctoral program in music education.

One course I found particularly interesting focused on different learning styles. How people learn has always been a fascination for me. Another course I really liked was called project planning – a semester-long process of developing a long-term project and charting when the different parts of this project had to begin, end, and so on. I loved the highly structured nature of the course.

Throughout my coursework, my academic career was carefully planned to fit my work schedule as an instructor of computer and business courses at other colleges. Using a technique I called "time shifting," I would make an agreement with the professor to take his or her course during the summer and register to receive the credits the following semester. This allowed me to work on academics during the summer months when I was not as busy teaching. My professors were impressed with my work and I obtained a grade point average of 3.83 out of a maximum of 4.0.

As far as I could tell, all my instructors were pleased with my work save a rather famous professor of music education who served as chair of music education. Something about the chemistry between us did not work. Contrary to the rest of the faculty, he felt that I was incompetent to be a doctoral student. He made my life miserable as, on several occasions, he attempted to remove my financial aid and in general devalued my work. A very political man, he did the same to other students. Eventually, he created so much consternation within the school of music that he was ordered out of the department.

> From this example and others, it appears that there are two major kinds of people who make a difference to my success and general well-being. The first includes those who like me and appreciate me for who I am despite any differences I may have. These people are helpful and try to protect me from bullies with whom I come in contact. The second group are those who seem to need to bully me in some way. The notion of these two groups of people was driven home at a conference where Anthony Attwood was the keynote speaker. As part of his presentation, Attwood outlined the two major responses people have to those with Asperger Syndrome: The protector/nurturer and the bully.
>
> A student with autism is enrolled in a college-level computer class I teach. I find this bully-nurturer paradigm applies to this person too. There are occasional impulsive outbursts

of comments and questions. His voice is often too loud and very flat. He is a good student and gets most of the questions correct. Most of the other students seem to realize that he is not "normal." A few students, however, appear very protective of him and encourage him to do the best he can. Nobody bullied him in this class, but some of his classmates didn't have much patience and rolled their eyes or exchanged looks when he acted inappropriately.

The doctoral program moved along well until it was time for me to sit for a series of five doctoral qualifier exams. Students are required to pass all of them before being allowed to begin work on their dissertation. My failure to pass on the first attempt was due to some careless mistakes in the music history exam. However, the problems in music theory were more significant.

My difficulties centered on a relative looseness of formal and tonal structure of Romantic music as compared to music of other periods. A composer uses a set of techniques to indicate when a piece of music has progressed from one section to the other. In the earlier music of composers such as Bach, Mozart and Beethoven, these devices occur at nearly the same time. In Romantic music some of the devices are employed earlier or later than in previous periods. While this lends much richness to the music, the relative looseness of the formal and tonal aspects of the music makes it difficult for me to analyze. Even though some of my favorite music is from the Romantic era, I feel lost in a sea of nonharmonic tones and am unable to impose an analytic structure upon the music.

Part of me felt very stupid for not being able to analyze music of the Romantics. A small part of me wondered if there was something of the past that was interfering with my ability to analyze Romantic music at a level that would satisfy the school of music. With these thoughts in mind, I underwent a psychoneurological test to learn more about my learning styles.

The results of the test indicated that I was performing in the well-above-average range overall, with some problem consistent with the "mild residual symptoms of autism." Performance on tasks based on visual learning such as identifying broken-up pieces of an object or recreating geometric designs was good. However, language-based problems such as memorizing a list of seemingly unrelated items and putting a series of pictures in the proper order were more difficult. In addition, difficulties in dealing with unstructured information and facial recognition were evident.

> *... The relative difficulties observed appear to be long-standing, and they are consistent with mild residual symptoms of autism. While Mr. Shore has outgrown or overcome most of the effects of this disorder and has done remarkably well in his life, the subtle difficulties that remain become significant when he is in situations that stress his weaknesses ...*

In addition to the summary below, the report included recommendations for accommodating my difficulties with music of the Romantic era.

> *... As noted on the formal data sheet, testing reveals significant neurocognitive deficits that are 1.5 or more standard deviations below Mr. Shore's overall intellectual capability, a requirement for a formal learning disorder. Given that Mr. Shore had a formal diagnosis of autism in childhood, he presents with a pervasive developmental disorder, which leads to atypical patterns of brain development. Problems with organization are residuals of autism that may be incompletely assessed in a structured testing environment. Thus, current testing may underassess Mr. Shore's organizational problems in unstructured educational settings.*

Given the above, accommodations and strategies for students with learning difficulties are recommended. In particular, the following educational accommodations will be helpful:

a. Examinations should be modified to allow Mr. Shore to better demonstrate his knowledge and mastery of the material. For example, for each question that requires dealing with unstructured information, an extra question might be added that allows him to work with more organized information. As seen on the California Verbal Learning Test and the Weschler Memory Scale-Revised Logical Memories subtest, material that is not organized is much more difficult for Mr. Shore than structured material.

b. Tutoring to help Mr. Shore learn to organize unstructured information (perhaps focusing on Romantic music) may prove very helpful.

c. Information should be presented visually whenever possible, as Mr. Shore learns extremely well when he sees the information. He has more difficulty when he must learn based on what he hears. This is seen on the Weschler Memory Scale-Revised subtests and on the California Verbal Learning Test.

d. Mr. Shore also learns remarkably well through practice and repetition, as seen across a variety of tasks including the Block Design and Digit Symbol subtests of the Weschler Adult Intelligence Scale-Revised. Thus he might benefit from finding ways to have important information repeated and presented in multiple modalities (e.g., visual, auditory).

Upon reviewing these results, I agreed with the doctor's recommendation that the report be sent to the Disability Services Office, which works with students in need of accommodation at the university. Soon thereafter, I met with a counselor, who said that upon receiving the report a letter would be sent to my advisor in the music education department. I stressed that I would prefer that the report with its recommendations first go to my advisor before reaching the department of music theory.

With much trepidation I subsequently disclosed to my advisor what I thought lay behind my difficulties with music of the Romantic era and told him that he would soon receive a report from the Disability Services Office. He was surprised when I told him of my past with autism and said he never would have guessed.

My advisor listened with much interest and an open mind. His comment "I never would have known" about my position on the autism spectrum seemed strange to me as I felt that he, without my telling him, would have no way of knowing of my diagnosis. On February 8, 2000, I recounted this conversation to Dr. Ann Roberts, the clinical psychologist at the Higashi School for Autism of Boston. At this point I had known Dr. Roberts for about two years. Since I had done observations and autobiographical presentations at this school, Ann knew of my quest for researching deeply about autism. She and I have become friends and plan to collaborate on writing some articles.

Dr. Roberts enlightened me that the response by my adviser was classified as a "carrier statement." These statements often carry far more weight and meaning than the face value of words. Like idioms, carrier statements are often difficult for people on the autism spectrum because of the need to infer meaning beyond the concrete words that make up the statement. Even a comment such as "that is very kind of you" or "that is very sweet" after I give someone a compliment seems strange to me. If I tell someone he did well on something, it's because I really think he did a good job. For me it's a statement of fact that I think something was well done and is deserving of me saying so. I don't give compliments in an effort to "be nice" or "be sweet" to another person.

Overall my advisor was very supportive but he warned me that while he would do his best to help, the final decision rested with the department of theory. Later that week I spoke with another professor in the music department who had been my advisor in the past. As before, she was also supportive of me.

The Three Modes of World

This experience of disclosing my history on the autism spectrum reverberated through my mind for a long time. With the help of "The three worlds of being" by Rollo May (1983) (see page 131), I slowly began to realize that there is a lot more to disclosure than merely stating "I have Asperger Syndrome." Disclosure involves three different facets of simultaneous existence. Translating from the German terms used by Rollo May, these concurrent worlds of existence are the "biological self," "being with myself," and "being with others."

The "biological self" is "the reality of the natural world" (May, 1983, p. 126). For me, this facet of being includes the color of my hair and eyes, gender, as well as perceptual, cognitive and affective strengths and weaknesses. Some of them include sensory sensitivities and integration issues. For me, this refers to my strong visual and mechanical abilities along with my difficulties in subtle social situations, recognizing faces and integrating unstructured information. For others on the autism spectrum, it may mean not being able to tolerate the humming and flickering of fluorescent lights or the sound of the blender emanating from the kitchen of the restaurant they are eating in.

The "being with myself" facet of existence revolves around a person's awareness of self. To me, this meant dealing with the fact that I had an imperfect ability to analyze music from the Romantic

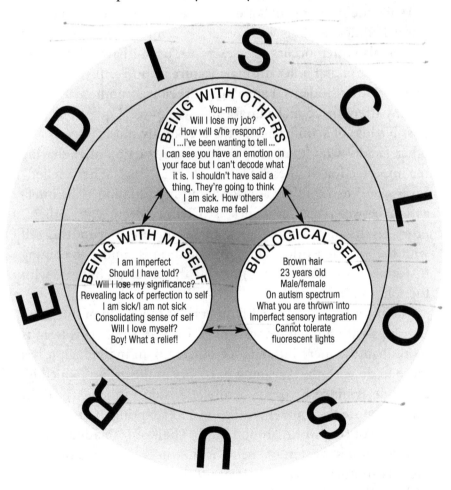

BEING WITH OTHERS
You-me
Will I lose my job?
How will s/he respond?
I ...I've been wanting to tell ...
I can see you have an emotion on your face but I can't decode what it is. I shouldn't have said a thing. They're going to think I am sick. How others make me feel

BEING WITH MYSELF
I am imperfect
Should I have told?
Will I lose my significance?
Revealing lack of perfection to self
I am sick/I am not sick
Consolidating sense of self
Will I love myself?
Boy! What a relief!

BIOLOGICAL SELF
Brown hair
23 years old
Male/female
On autism spectrum
What you are thrown into
Imperfect sensory integration
Cannot tolerate
fluorescent lights

This diagram was developed from the work of May, R. (1983), Chapter Nine. "The three modes of world." *The discovery of being: Writings in existential psychology*. New York: W.W. Norton, pp. 126-132. In this chapter he writes about the simultaneous existence of three worlds entitled *Mitwelt* (being with others), *Eigenwelt* (self-awareness through self-conversation), and *Umwelt* (the world around one).

era compared to what the doctoral program considered as "normal" and, moreover, I had to share that with another human being. Although grappling with ideas of imperfection or differences was enlightening to me as I set out to make the disclosure, the process of revealing the imperfection was painful. Some people, including myself, use this experience as a launching pad to help others working through the same issues.

While the primary goal of disclosure usually is to reach better mutual understanding with others, a better understanding of oneself also often occurs. For example, once I have admitted to myself that taking notes during a lecture is more difficult for me than for other students, I am able to develop accommodations to use my strengths to make up for this weakness. I questioned my possible loss of significance in the eyes of my music advisor and other faculty who knew me. A common reaction after sharing the imperfection of oneself with another is "Boy! What a relief!" I was glad I had told my advisor about my situation. The interaction between the "biological self" and "being with others" often results in a consolidation of self before sharing this self with the outside world. This consolidation is similar to coming to a supervisor at work with not only the problem, but also with the solution in hand.

The third facet, "Being with others," "is the world of interrelationships with human beings" (May, 1983, p. 127). This term is more than the mere influence of others on an individual; it has more to do with the "meaning of others in the group [which is] partly determined by one's own relationship to them" (p. 127). There is more than merely adjusting and adapting in the biological sense of the "world around one." The word "relationship" is a more apt description of "being with others." In a relationship there is mutual awareness (May, 1983). During an encounter with another human, both persons change as a result.

"Being with others" with mutual awareness can be the most difficult part of disclosure for the person on the autism spectrum.

A lot of communication between people involves nonverbal communication such as eye contact, facial expressions and body language. As a result, the person with autism or Asperger Syndrome may not be able to detect the very changes in a relationship they are trying to effect with disclosure unless the other person verbalizes in clear terms that the communication has been effective. Denial of one's differences and imperfections is another common reaction to the facets of "being with myself" and "being with others."

Several months went by without any information from the Disability Services Office. Repeated calls revealed that the office had yet to do anything with my report. And, as a result, the School of Music had received nothing on this matter.

After a few more months I received a letter from the Disability Services Office stating that my request for accommodation had been rejected. The rationale for the rejection was that all music theory was highly structured. They had missed the boat. The fact that music theory is highly structured was not the concern. The concern centered on the music itself, which, as acknowledged by the chair of theory, can be unstructured.

With this letter in hand I spoke to my advisor. He had not been contacted by the Disability Services Office as they had promised. Instead, a letter had gone directly to the chair of theory for consideration. Had I known that, I would have disclosed my situation to this person before the letter arrived.

Not being able to get anywhere, I contacted the doctor who had administered the neuropsychological exam. She understood the problem and promised to personally go to the Disability Services Office and talk with the director. Before doing so, she requested that I write her a letter describing my situation and the miscommunication between the office and the department of music theory.

> ... [T]he Disability Services Office has chosen to focus on music theory as the issue instead of analysis of music of the Romantic era, as we had requested.
>
> It appears that [the] chairperson of theory and composition in the School for the Arts was contacted. She stated
>
> > ... there is no difference between Romantic era music theory and any other era's music theory, and noted that although the music of this period was often unstructured, the theory of this period was highly structured.
>
> While what [the chair of music theory] said is entirely true, it is the music of the Romantic era that is the issue, as opposed to music theory itself ... The relative lack of structure in music of the Romantic era conflicts with my learning issues and makes it difficult for me to find this and other musical events ...

Insofar as the music theory itself, there is no problem as it is highly structured, as the chair of the music department indicated. Musical events are signified with similar theoretical notation for all eras of music. The devices used to indicate a major structural change can include changes in tempo, harmony, melody, volume and orchestration. In music of earlier eras, these devices all occur at pretty much the same time. The composition reaches its next structural area when these devices are all worked out. In the case of Romantic music, these devices occur at varying times with some occurring earlier or later than in previous eras. The resultant muddiness in the demarcation of the structural borders along with the increased use of tones that are not part of a given chord make it more difficult for me to separate the foreground from the background in order to determine the harmony.

Despite the support from my advisor and others, along with a fairly mild request for accommodations, the department of theory only allowed me to repeat courses and audit additional courses as needed. The Disability Services Office could only offer me a counselor to help structure my time but not one who specialized in music theory. These accommodations felt useless since I received good grades and encouragement from the theory courses I had taken.

> About two years later I received an e-mail from the director of the Disability Services Office, who wrote that she found my book fascinating and would like to meet with me in her office to talk further. Although the identifying information in the book had been omitted or changed for confidentiality, apparently people who were involved in the situation had recognized themselves. Unsure of what she wanted, I made the appointment.

> I was pleasantly surprised to find the director apologizing for not understanding my situation better at the time. She added that she would have advocated for me more strongly if she had known then what she knows now—her son had just been diagnosed with Asperger Syndrome! Now, as good friends, she and I present at national conferences together and often share this story at our talks.

Seeing my dream of earning a doctorate in music slip away, combined with the time and energy I had invested in the program, was very upsetting. During my high school years, I would go to music stores and look at college music students purchasing scores to beloved pieces of music with wonderment. Nothing was more noble to me than majoring in music. In almost all cases, a requirement for attaining my goal of full-time employment in higher education is the completion of a terminal degree in the subject. With the loss of the music teaching position at the college, it became clear that the goal of teaching music in higher education needed to be reworked into something else.

It was time to register for the qualifier exams again. Although my chances of passing this hurdle were slim, part of me wanted to shoot this mad wounded horse of a terminal degree in music and be done with it. My music advisor had stopped me cold and suggested I consider continuing doctoral studies at a school of education. He explained that in addition to being painful emotionally, the results of failing this exam might show up on my academic record with my work towards this degree being nullified.

The convergence of the loss of my music faculty position with the difficulties of meeting the requirements of the music qualifier exam, and my growing interest in autism, seemed to point towards doing doctoral work in an area related to this disability. Consequently, I applied to doctoral programs of education at two major universities in the Boston area. Both institutions had programs aligned with my proposed course of study and encouraged me to apply. However, after meeting with the chair of special education at Boston University, I felt more of a connection there.

In my applications I declared an interest in working with college students having mild disabilities, possibly undiagnosed, yet likely to be disruptive to their learning processes. Based on my recent experiences, I felt it was necessary to make the admissions committee fully aware of the origins of my interests in autism and learning processes. With much conviction and some trepidation, I made full disclosure of my relationship to the autism spectrum and how it had led to my interest in this area of higher education. I even included a then current draft of this book.

Disclosing my relationship to the autism spectrum was very important at this time because it directly affected my upcoming entrance into the world of special education and the autism spectrum. In addition, after going through the experience with the music degree, I felt it was of the utmost importance to be up front in disclosing my disability, even if it involved negative effects on my application decision. Even though people with disabilities are often considered less capable and are given less of a chance to succeed than a person without the apparent disability in similar circumstances (Goffman, 1963), I was striving for two main effects.

The first, and more obvious one, was for a positive change in my potential future relationship with the school that would accept me. However, a more subtle, larger effect remains. That effect relates to the change in the societal construction of a person on the autism spectrum. Each individual disclosure works towards changing this societal construct one person at a time. This change in societal construction is evident over the long term. For example, during the 1950s and 1960s autism was considered to be of psychological origin caused by a reflection by the child of rejection from the mother (Bettelheim, 1967; Dolnick, 1998). This belief was challenged in the mid-1960s and early 1970s by Dr. Bernard Rimland (1964), who set out to prove a biological basis to this disorder.

Autobiographies and accounts about people on the autism spectrum began to appear in the 1960s and 1970s (Kaufman, 1976; Park, 1967). These stories of disclosure began to move the societal construct of the person on the autism spectrum from the nonverbal, antisocial, self-abusive child flapping his hands in the corner of the room to somebody who is capable of contributing to society. The 1990s brought an explosion of information about autism via the Internet and more autobiographies (Grandin, 1995; Johnson & Crowder, 1994; Sellin, 1995; Willey, 1999; Williams, 1992) by people on the autism spectrum. According to the Autism Resources web site by Jim Wobus (2000), from 1935 to 1959 only three nonfiction books were written about autism. This increased to 24 in the 1960s, 78 in the 1970s, 129 in the 1980s and a phenomenal increase to 338 in the 1990s. This boom in nonfiction reading material on autism helps make society more tolerant and appreciative of the contributions people on the autism spectrum can make. The acceptance of autism in society, in turn, encourages more writing about this subject with a corresponding decrease in the stigma attached to the disorder.

The second effect of disclosure relates to society as a whole. Each disclosure about a disability that results in deeper mutual understanding changes not only the disclosee's construct of the disorder but potentially that of everyone else with whom the disclosee comes in contact. With luck, the disclosee can act as sort of an ambassador and relay this information to others. For the most part, disclosure is a one-to-one personal event with the goal of better mutual understanding. Possibly the person who has been disclosed to can carry forward this information to others at appropriate times and manners. However, disclosure via articles, autobiographies, and presentations reaches a wider audience more quickly. In short, disclosure defines for the public construct what autism is and how to have better mutual relationships with people having autism. The disclosure conference hosted by the Asperger's Association of New England on 11 March, 2000, was the first event ever devoted solely to the issues surrounding disclosure. More such "mass" communications of this important issue will speed positive change in public constructs of the autism spectrum.

While working through the theories and issues surrounding disclosure is interesting to me, I remained apprehensive about my full disclosure to the schools I had applied to. Hopefully at least one of the schools would be able to see beyond the autism spectrum disorder to the person seeking further education in this area.

I was pleasantly surprised to receive acceptance to the doctoral program in special education at Boston University. Whereas I had had so much trouble receiving accommodation at the doctoral level in music, I was welcomed with open arms to the school of education to study special education. Finally, I would be able to refocus my energies on an area of study that is important to me. With my concerns about funding my work melting away upon the award of a scholarship sufficient to cover most of tuition, it felt like the right thing to do.

While the college experience is often very positive and liberating for people on the autism spectrum, higher education can pose many challenges. More about successfully planning for and remaining in college can be found in Appendix B, "Getting Ready for College."

CHAPTER TWELVE

Revisiting the Castle

I n the summer of 1996, while deeply involved in both teaching at the college and in the doctoral music program, my mother called to tell me about a book on autism she had just read. She was reluctant to tell me about it because she was afraid that if I read it I might feel bad about myself. I told her that I would read the book and at least find out more about myself and reassured her that I was willing to take on any risks of feeling bad about myself. The book was *Thinking in Pictures and Other Reports from My Life with Autism* by Dr. Temple Grandin. As usual, my mother had made annotations in the book where certain traits Dr. Grandin described pertained to her. I went through the book and did the same but in another color.

As I read the text, I felt that Temple Grandin validated feelings I had about myself. The sleeping dragon of autism awoke and I began to read other texts on the subject at used bookstores with a trusted friend of many years who is also interested in psychology and cognitive development. Reading these books was difficult, sometimes to the point of causing knots in my stomach as I perused the pages. Previous to this time I had been aware of my past. My parents never hid it from me and we talked openly about it from time to time. But I probably thought about autism no more often than once every six months.

Around this time, this friend mentioned an upcoming presentation on autism by Temple Grandin in Cambridge. Although he was unable to attend, I was not letting anything get in the way of my going.

Even before Temple Grandin's lecture started, this turned out to be a wonderful experience. A person sitting next to me in the audience mentioned her work with children who have autism. Her name was Susan Zurawski. Upon learning that she worked at the Language and Cognitive Development Center in Jamaica Plain, I asked if I could come and observe some time. I told her of my personal involvement with the autism spectrum and that I would like to find out more about it. She agreed to my request.

The lecture was interesting. Even though I knew all of the quotes that she read from her book, meeting Dr. Grandin was a memorable experience. The "personal" encounter during the booksigning following the presentation lasted only 30 seconds. Standing in line to get my book signed, I asked one of the "handlers" how I might communicate with Temple Grandin. As she started to explain that I could reach her through the publisher, Temple herself suddenly looked up and exclaimed in a matter-of-fact voice, "What do you want to communicate with me about?" I told her that I had a personal history with autism and thanked her for making more people aware of what autism is. She asked what I did for a living and when I told her I taught music and computers at the college level, she said "That's a good thing to do." Then she immediately changed gears to continue signing books.

> I met Temple Grandin again three years after she gave her presentation on autism. At that time there were no "handlers" next to her and we had a longer conversation about my using music and computers to work with children across the autism spectrum and about my writing this autobiography.

Reconnecting with Temple Grandin

Even after being in contact with Temple three or four times, I was never able to truly strike up what I felt was a meaningful conversation with her. In fairness to Temple, I may have caught her at times when she was not in a mood to talk after a long day of traveling and presenting.

This changed in the fall of 2002 when I presented on disclosure for people on the autism spectrum at a MAAP conference (More Advanced Individuals with Autism, Asperger's Syndrome and Pervasive Developmental Disorders). Temple had delivered a keynote address the night before, and the following morning as I was looking for a place to eat breakfast, I noticed her distinctive cowboy shirt from the rear. Walking past Temple into her field of vision so as not to startle her, I said hello. Immediately inviting me to join her for breakfast, she stated that she was glad that "someone from the conference had come to sit with her." What an opportunity to talk one on one with someone whom I often think of as the "grandmother" of autism; that is, the first person to widely publish and present about her position on the autism spectrum. We talked about a myriad things. One of them was the analogy between feeling lost when analyzing music from the Romantic era due to its relative ambiguity of structure and not being able to define the edge of our breakfast table if a piece of plywood was placed on top to extend its width. Temple built on the analogy by adding a tablecloth on top of the now enlarged table surface causing one to not even wonder where the true edge of the table was because it was impossible to see the modification. Like with the relative looseness of structure in music of the Romantic era, it's difficult to know where the boundary of the table truly is, especially with the added tablecloth. What a visual thinker! Temple tells it like it is. No more and no less. Very refreshing.

The next week I went to the Language and Cognitive Development Center (LCDC) to observe Susan at work. After a tour of the school I was left in the observation room. I immediately felt a good energy about the school. There was an openness to anyone who was interested in observing their work. I later found out that parents are invited to observe from the observation rooms at any time. This is important since working with a child with autism has to be a cooperative venture between the parents, school and anyone else who is involved.

Cyberspace for People Like Me

I had been a subscriber to America Online for quite a while and was serving as a host of Classical Chat. After some exploring, I located an autism chat room run by the director of the League School of Greater Boston, Herman Fishbein. Through this experience I met many people who were very interested in my history. One I met in person, Laurie Smith. As director of a special education program on the North Shore of Massachusetts, Laurie worked with young children on the autistic spectrum. After we began to communicate more via chatrooms and instant messages I asked whether I might observe her teach. I had heard horror stories of people meeting in real life after getting to know each other in cyberspace, but we both figured that anyone involved in autism would probably be OK, so we agreed to meet.

Cyberspace can be a good place for those on the autistic spectrum to meet others. For example, I have been invited to present at several conferences as a direct result of my cyberspace connections. There are a number of reasons for the advantages of cyberspace to individuals with autism. The communication bandwidth is restricted to text. As a result, there are none of the nonverbal aspects of communication that so often present difficulties for those on the autistic spectrum. Also, there are no distractions of trying to remember what someone's face looks like or what they might be trying to say via body language or tone of voice. Finally, if you no longer wish to communicate with a certain person, he or she can be ignored.

Live communication between people consists of two major channels or domains: verbal and nonverbal. Verbal communication refers to speech, or with a computer, it is the typed-out text that appears on the computer screen. Nonverbal communication includes tone of voice, facial expressions and body language.

With most people, the nonverbal communication supplements or enhances the verbal communication. The two channels are processed together to give a deeper meaning to the communication. With people having autism and Asperger Syndrome, however, the nonverbal component can be so difficult to decode that it interferes with getting meaning from the verbal channel. As a result, very little, if any, communication occurs. This may be one reason why many people on the autism spectrum avoid eye contact when maintaining a conversation. The energy involved in reading the nonverbal data may interfere with getting the meaning from the verbal data.

There are times when I feel that communicating with computers is easier than talking with people. This becomes especially clear when someone asks me how to do something on the computer. Often when I try to explain it, I get stuck, but if I grab the mouse and keyboard, performing the needed task is very easy. Then I can run through what I did in my mind and explain what I did. It is much easier for me to show what to do than to verbalize the process.

I am able to teach computers at the college level because I prepare myself by running through the procedures first so I have a "virtual computer" in my mind as I explain the steps to my students. If I get asked how to do something that I haven't prepared, I quickly run through the steps on a computer before explaining it.

During my time as a professor of music and computers, I found many students with disabilities attracted to both my music and computer courses as these courses gave them an avenue where they could excel. The computer is patient and makes it easy to correct mistakes. In many ways, the computer can act as an assistive device that allows a person to concentrate on the content of a particular matter rather than getting bogged down with the details of writing neatly or making drawings relate to what is pictured in one's mind.

> The computer serves as a wonderful assistive device for me. My fine-motor skills for writing and drawing are somewhat impaired. As a result, creating a neat handwritten document is labor-intensive and time-consuming for me. Given that I have some ability to communicate with the computer via the keyboard, I can create documents that look much better in much less time. The relative ease of creating a good-looking document may determine whether the document is produced at all rather than being considered as something that will be too arduous to create.

Employment using computers is often a good avenue for individuals with autism or Asperger Syndrome. I might have gone into computer programming; however, I was scared away from the mathematics requirements based on my first-grade teacher announcing that I would never be able to do math, as stated earlier. Although algebra can be difficult for me due to the need to keep more than one variable in mind, I did well in a college calculus course and enjoy statistical analysis. And, as mentioned before, I have taught these subjects at the college level.

However, there are still the social challenges of the workplace. The question of disclosing one's association with autism or any other disability is a very serious one requiring much thought.

The reactions from employers can range from utter fear of having a monster in the work setting to acceptance and a willingness to accommodate the person with a disability. Since autism and other cognitive disabilities are invisible, the challenge of getting a positive reaction to self-disclosure is greater than for other disabilities.

The person on the higher end of the autism spectrum must often contend with being somewhere between the visible and invisible type of disability. Others may sense there is something different but they cannot quite figure out what it is. For example, after disclosing the reasons behind my unusually strong interest in autism to a colleague of mine, she responded, "I've had my eye on you and wondered what was going on." This person had extensive experience in special education and consequently was aware of various disorders. Others, including my wife, "noticed something" when we first met but could not determine what that "something" was. Disclosure is usually best accomplished by the person with the disorder as he or she is most aware of the issues. However, sometimes it is appropriate for another person who is knowledgeable about the situation to either break the groundwork for disclosure or do the disclosing itself. One reason for having another person do the disclosure is that the person with the disorder may for some reason be unable to do it – perhaps the stress of disclosing would cause his or her verbal abilities to be impaired or shut down.

According to Erving Goffman in *Stigma: Notes on the Management of Spoiled Identity* (1963), those with invisible disabilities are not immediately discredited but bear the burden of becoming discreditable. That is, they often go about life holding the disorder a secret while possibly revealing it to a few select close others. Revealing an invisible disability to somebody else, particularly if it is somebody the person has known for a while, often presents greater difficulties than dealing with a visible disability that is "up close and center." The disclosee may wonder why this information has been withheld up to this point. As mentioned earlier, my wife wondered why I had waited several years before revealing to her my relationship to the autism spectrum.

YOUR STREET ADDRESS
YOUR TOWN, YOUR STATE ZIP CODE
CURRENT DATE

Ms. Jane Doe
ABC Company
1234 First Street
City, State 12345

Dear Ms. Doe:

Thank you very much for giving me the opportunity to work for ABC Company. I am looking forward to beginning work, and will try hard to understand and fulfill all my job responsibilities. In this letter, I would like to offer you some important personal information that may affect how I perform in my new job. As you may already know, I have Asperger Syndrome (AS for short). It may be helpful if you, as my supervisor at ABC Company, understand some characteristics of AS. This will help you make some accommodations for my different learning style, so that I can become a good employee who will contribute to ABC Company's success.

Asperger Syndrome is a form of autism characterized by normal to superior IQ, accompanied by social and communication difficulties. These difficulties stem from neurologically based sensory- and information-processing disabilities. Even though I may look just like everybody else, my mind works in a significantly different way, and sometimes my behavior and reactions are not typical.

There is wide variation in the abilities and personalities of individuals with AS, but we do have a lot in common. For example, it is likely I will not understand office politics. I may occasionally lose my cool, or "put my foot in my mouth." On the positive side, I am honest and good-hearted. Once I understand the tasks and routines necessary to my job, I will perform them faithfully. With skillful supervision, you can minimize the impact of my weaknesses and make the best use of my many strengths. Here is a list of the kinds of accommodations that could help me feel comfortable and be a good employee. It would help if you, as my supervisor, can:

- Give me a *written* job description that spells out all my responsibilities in detail.
- Give me a written daily/weekly schedule.
- Give me specific, detailed instructions for each new task you assign to me.
- Present all new information *in writing*, rather than just orally.
- Give me a *little extra time* or coaching to master a new task or absorb new information.
- Give me an explicit, detailed list of rules governing workplace protocol around such matters as dress, timing and length of breaks, and when and where conversation with other employees is allowed. (I will probably *not* be able to intuit these rules for myself.)
- Train me thoroughly in the correct operation and rules for use of any workplace machinery or equipment such as copiers, postage meters, the telephone system, and fax machines.
- If possible, meet with me briefly at the beginning of each day to review the day's agenda and to forewarn me about any upcoming changes in the schedule/routine. (If more convenient, we could meet at the end of each day to preview the next workday.) I may have trouble handling abrupt transitions or surprises, but can adapt well if I am forewarned.

- Let me know to whom I should turn (and when and how) with questions or problems – to you, and/or to an empathetic person in the personnel office, or to a job coach or a Rehabilitation staff person.
- Try to allow me to focus on and complete one task at a time. If an interruption is unavoidable, please allow me a short time to adjust. (If I am interrupted suddenly, I may become anxious, and then I may do or say something inappropriate. I do not intend to be rude – I may just be neurologically overwhelmed. If this happens, please give me a chance to take a break and calm myself. Later we can discuss how to handle similar situations better.)
- Try to avoid assigning me tasks with pressing deadlines, difficult personalities to deal with, or other factors that can ignite my anxieties.
- Understand that even though I may not make eye contact while you are speaking to me, I am listening to you. (It is hard for me to process auditory and visual information simultaneously.)
- Meet with me regularly and frequently to let me know how I am doing. Acknowledge whatever I am doing well. If you need to give negative feedback, the most effective approach is to suggest in a calm and neutral way any concrete steps I can take to correct the mistakes. (Due to our disability, people with AS have trouble understanding other people's viewpoints. For example, I may sometimes say things that are unintentionally hurtful or abrupt. I may need your feedback to realize this behavior is inappropriate and replace it with more acceptable behavior.)
- Recognize and accept my social or sensory limitations. Limit the amount of contact I have with the general public, and the amount of time I must interact with large groups or work in noisy settings. After working with a group, I may need a "sensory break" – a walk to the mailbox, or some time working alone at a task in a quiet part of the office.
- Be patient and flexible. If you give directions and feedback calmly, I will feel less anxious, and can perform my best work for you.
- Help me decide if others in the company should also know I have AS. If personnel officers and coworkers can be understanding and accepting, they can help me succeed.
- Be compassionate. I have met with a lot of misunderstanding and failure in the past, despite my best efforts to meet society's expectations. Although I may not always remember to express my thanks verbally, I will reward your patient supervisory efforts with a solid, reliable work performance.

Some employees with AS need outside support to adjust to a new work environment. I know you have many other responsibilities, so if I seem to need more support than you can readily provide, you may wish to get some outside help. Examples of organizations to contact include the Asperger Syndrome Coalition of the United States, Asperger Syndrome Education Network, and More Advanced Individuals with Autism, Asperger's Syndrome and Pervasive Developmental Disorders (MAAP).

Thank you very much for taking the time to think about this important information. I look forward to working for you.

Sincerely,

YOUR NAME
Your new title

To help with the problem of disclosure in the workplace, I was asked to assist in developing a letter (pages 146-147) for the Asperger's Association of New England. The organization provides support in the form of information, conferences, and support groups for people associated with those with Asperger Syndrome as well as for individuals who have Asperger Syndrome. After serving on the board of directors, I presently serve as president of the board of this organization.

The Language and Cognitive Development Center

My observations at LCDC continued. So far, my time at the school had been spent behind a glass window of an observation room followed by discussions of the day's events with Susan after the children went home.

The day I became an involuntary volunteer was a turning point. Susan said, "I usually don't do this but would you like to observe from inside the room instead of from behind the glass?" I was a bit nervous to accept the offer because I thought it might interfere with the class. Also, what would I do if a child came over to me and acted out in some manner?

> As a student teacher at the middle school level, I had found that I had problems with classroom management. Quite often I couldn't seem to get the students to understand and follow what I wanted them to do. When I interned at an elementary school in Chelsea, Massachusetts, the children sometimes ran absolutely wild. Thinking back to that time, this problem was confined to a particular first-grade classroom that had a reputation for including children with challenging behaviors. However, I remember another teacher coming in and somehow getting them to quiet down. I felt as if there was a communication barrier between these elementary-school children and me that I couldn't break through.

The challenge I just described stems at least partly from the fact that my development during primary school was atypical. Since I did not experience typical interactions with my schoolmates, I lacked a basis upon which to develop a positive teaching relationship upon returning to the classroom as a student teacher. I believe that starting with middle school, and certainly by college, I had enough awareness of myself in relation to others that I could be successful in teaching at the college level. Although I did not understand the protocol for interacting with typical children in elementary school, I quickly found it easy for me to relate to the children at the Language and Cognitive Development Center.

All this went through my mind as I considered Susan's offer. Taking a deep breath and facing the risk that something unpleasant might happen, I agreed.

On the first day I sat as far in the corner as possible trying to make myself invisible. Not five minutes had passed before Susan asked me to put the shoes on one of the children's feet. That didn't seem so bad. The rest of the morning passed quickly as I helped in the classroom. I had become an involuntary volunteer and it felt good. From that time on, I have been serving as a volunteer at the Center one or more days a week.

The students spend most of their time in a classroom setting where the average ratio is one head teacher and two aides for six children. Students get pulled out of the classroom for various therapies in cognitive development, speech, woodshop, computer, and so on. I found the individual cognitive interventions very interesting and volunteered in these sessions.

At this time I was not familiar with Miller Method Theory. I didn't even know that Dr. Miller was the director of the school but it felt to me that what Susan, the teacher, and the others did with these children was *right*.

One part of the program at LCDC consisted of individual cognitive sessions. A number of repetitive tasks were laid out in areas or stations of the room, which the child had to accomplish. For example, standing next to a small stair-case that led to a slide and holding a sign that said "Up," I would say the word and point upwards at the same time to the child, who would climb the stairs, sit down and go down the slide.

Following this, the child would go to a trampoline and fall onto it as the therapist said, "Alex falls down!" After he had jumped for a short while, the therapist would exclaim "stop!" and stop Alex from jumping. Michael Biundo, the psychologist who designed this cognitive-developmental session, then tried to get Alex to sway from side to side with him in an imitative manner. I noticed that Dr. Biundo's voice would rise and fall a minor third every time he said "side-side." I have found that most successful therapists talk to the students in a musical tone. For example, when telling a child to "sit down," the voice drops a minor third on the word "down." This is the same interval used by a doorbell when it makes the "ding-dong" sound. Considered the easiest melodic interval to sing by music scholars such as the late Leonard Bernstein (1973), it is also found in the first two syllables of the "nyah nyah nyah nyah nyah" taunt sung by children in many parts of the world.

Then Alex would go to another station where he would have to pull on a rope attached to a truck that had a weight in it to provide more resistance to pulling. He would pick up the weight and have to place it into the appropriate-sized recep-tacle for this weight. There might be other activities in other areas of the room too.

Alex did all these activities in a round a few times before the task was expanded by additional requirements in order for him to complete the circuit. The child, the therapist, and I all had a good time during these sessions. Mike would continually tell Alex what he was doing as he did it. This type of narrating was done in all areas of the school.

The "board room" was another interesting place. Although it is tempting to call it a gym or an obstacle course, it was much more than that. Here the children would go through a circuit on elevated boards. At different points on the circuit, there would be stations where they had to complete some task. I liked the board room and often wished to play on the structures myself.

Work in LCDC is one of continual action. I noticed that no "time-out" was used to isolate a child who misbehaves. Instead, the emphasis is on finding out what in the environment causes the challenging behaviors. Upon asking Arnold Miller, the director of the program, about this, he responded that he could not see any benefit to isolating a child who is already isolated from the environment. The only time I saw a child removed from the room was during a particularly challenging period when the aide took the child out of the classroom to wash his face and explain in a matter-of-fact way what he should be doing. The idea of focusing on why a child is exhibiting challenging behaviors rather then just punishing her for the actions displayed is much more productive.

Meeting Dr. Arnold Miller

In my continued quest for information about autism and Asperger Syndrome on the Internet, I was surprised one day to find a link to the Language and Cognitive Development Center; I filled out a questionnaire requesting further information. I received an early-morning response, time stamped at 5:56 a.m., from Dr. Miller who, in addition to co-founding the school with his wife, Eileen Eller-Miller, serves as executive director. He expressed pleasure in my interest and invited me to make an appointment with him, which I promptly did.

I found Dr. Miller to be an interested and interesting person. He started out by inquiring about my interest in autism. I first gave him the "politically correct" answer and then told him the truth.

> Regrettably, many people still have misconceptions about limitations and capabilities of people on the autism spectrum. To those to whom I don't wish to disclose my history with autism, I mention that I got hooked on studying this disorder when I noticed how a small child with autism who avoided eye contact suddenly made eye contact with me as I played my flute for him. This comprises my "politically correct answer."

> Dr. Miller told me later that at the start of our initial phone conversation, I appeared to be "another academic looking for information on autism." Given that Dr. Miller is a developmental psychologist working in the field of autism, I felt that his greater understanding of the autism spectrum would make him a safer person to disclose to.

Dr. Miller was a very direct person, which I appreciate as it allows me to know where I stand with him. As I told him about my history, he suddenly commented, "You don't seem to be having any problems processing this conversation." To this I responded that while I felt I have managed to work through most of my difficulties associated with autism and Asperger Syndrome, I am left with some residual effects. Day-to-day functioning is fine as I have managed to make accommodations for most situations. However, difficulties remain in subtle social situations such as office politics.

Arnold Miller inquired whether I would do an autobiographical presentation for the LCDC staff, to which I agreed. By the time of my first presentation at LCDC, I had been volunteering there for about a year. Volunteering was important to me for two reasons. First, I hoped I could use my personal experiences with the autism spectrum to help the children. Second, by working with these children, I was able to bring back my own memories of when I was in a similar state.

Actually, my premier presentation on my personal experiences with autism took place at the Allegro School for Autistic Children at Cedar Knolls in northern New Jersey to parents and professionals in the field. Thanks to cyber-communication, I had made contact with others on the autism spectrum, which resulted in my being invited to present at the Allegro School for Autistic Children.

So, the talk at LCDC was my second presentation. But since it was my first at this school, I was a bit nervous. A large part of my nervousness stemmed from the fact that in contrast to the New Jersey presentation, this one was much closer to home and for people with whom I had regular contact. But despite the internal butterflies, the presentation turned out very well and I was promptly invited to give additional talks from time to time.

I was apprehensive about the kind of questions the audience might ask but I was secure in my knowledge that Dr. Miller and I had laid the groundwork beforehand. He would introduce me for what I am – a person diagnosed with strong autistic tendencies when younger and now teaching at the college level along with (at that time) finishing a doctoral degree in music education. The presentation would end with a question-and-answer session. It would be okay to ask any question as long as I reserved the right to state that "I am not comfortable talking about that at this time." Arnold Miller promised that he would make sure that the questions asked would be "appropriate" and step in if needed to provide support.

safe guards in
conversation
sharing

As it turned out, the staff and Dr. Miller asked good and appropriate questions. It was helpful to answer these questions as many of them forced me to think of my relationship with autism and Asperger Syndrome in new ways. An overall feeling of good energy, support and willingness to learn emanated from the people of the Language and Cognitive Development Center.

CHAPTER THIRTEEN

Challenging the Walls

How the Autistic Disorder Is now Classified

D isorders such as PDD-NOS, autism and Asperger
Syndrome (AS) are currently classified under a group of
disorders known as Pervasive Developmental Disorders
(PDD) by the *Diagnostic and Statistical Manual of Mental
Disorders of the American Psychiatric Association*, 4th edition, text
revision (DSM-IV). The diagnoses that fall under PDD exhibit
impairments in communication and social deficits, along with
restricted and repetitive interests and activities. However, these
attributes differ in terms of severity. The diagram on page 156, as
adapted from Bryna Siegel's *The World of the Autistic Child*
(1996, p. 10), shows where the autistic disorder fits into the
umbrella of the pervasive developmental diagnoses.

Autism Compared with Other Disorders

However, this depiction isolates autism from the diagnoses of
Asperger Syndrome and Pervasive Development Disorder-Not
Otherwise Specified and fails to describe what I feel are the true
relationships between these disorders. The way these diagnoses
are set up in the DSM IV, the autistic disorder appears as the
only one of the five diagnoses listed under the numerical category
of 299 as true autism. As a result, parents of children with

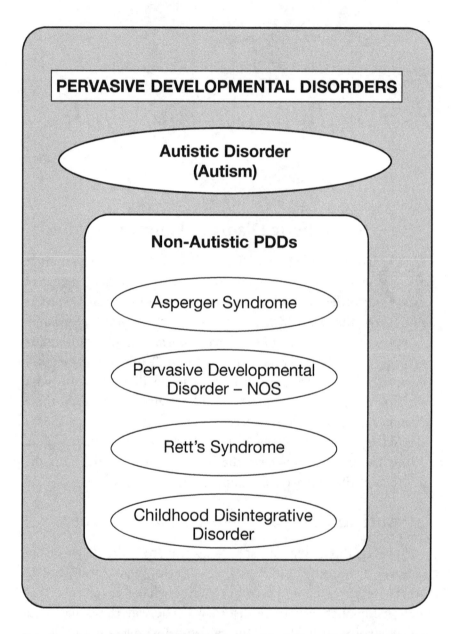

Developed from Siegel, B. (1996). *The world of the autistic child: Understanding and treating autistic spectrum disorders.* New York: Oxford University Press, p. 10. Printed with permission from Oxford University Press.

diagnoses of PDD-NOS and AS often consider their children not to have autism. According to the DSM IV, this is correct.

Addressing autism, Asperger Syndrome and Pervasive Developmental Disorder-Not Otherwise Specified by what they have in common makes it easier to understand their relationship to each other and the pervasive developmental disorder in general. These three diagnoses share the specific delays in social interaction, communication and restricted repetitive and stereotyped patterns of behavior, interests and activities.

PDD-NOS is often used as a catch-all in which to cast children who exhibit a certain number and severity of autistic traits. In my opinion, examiners using this classification often don't quite know where to place the child or want to protect parents and the child from the stigma of an autism diagnosis. But the reality is that an autism diagnosis will provide more services in many school municipalities and should therefore be used when appropriate.

Perhaps an even better way would be to place more emphasis on providing the services and program a child needs as opposed to getting caught up in which "brand" of autism is involved. To this end, considering autism as a spectrum disorder with varying degrees of severity and presentation may be of help.

The Autism Spectrum

When examining the criteria of these diagnoses in the DSM IV, it makes more sense to classify autism, PDD-NOS, and Asperger Syndrome as a separate category – the autism spectrum. Looking at these three disorders as part of the autism spectrum does more to bring them together based on their similarities than dividing them into distinct categories.

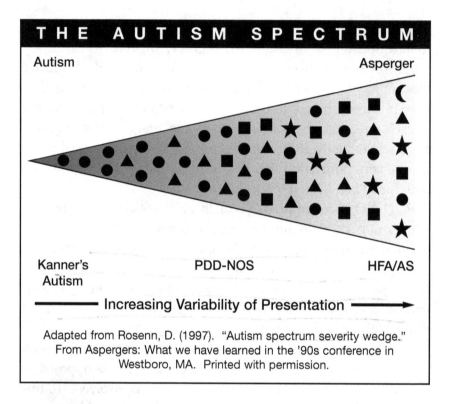

THE AUTISM SPECTRUM

Autism

Asperger

Kanner's Autism

PDD-NOS

HFA/AS

→ Increasing Variability of Presentation →

Adapted from Rosenn, D. (1997). "Autism spectrum severity wedge." From Aspergers: What we have learned in the '90s conference in Westboro, MA. Printed with permission.

This diagram, developed by Daniel Rosenn, M.D. (1997), shows autism as a spectrum disorder with different levels of severity and presentation. Considering autism as a continuum of its own may help solve the problems of defining and classifying people who are within the autism spectrum. The high-functioning Asperger portion of this syndrome has the greatest diversity in shapes because the variation in presentation along with the number of people with autism in this area is the greatest. At the extreme right, those with autism blend into the general population. This autism spectrum severity wedge diagram shows that it is impossible to state unequivocally that a person with autism must have a particular trait or cannot have another trait.[14]

---

[14] I am indebted to Dr. Daniel Rosenn for both granting me permission to use this graphic and for his explanation of its relation to the autism spectrum disorders.

There is a point where a person may move off the autism spectrum. The person still has the tendencies but may be considered an "autistic cousin." Coined by Autism Network International, the term "autistic cousin" refers to a person whose autistic tendencies are not strong nor numerous enough to be considered as belonging on the autism spectrum. However, as mentioned in Chapter Six, "Autistic Echoes," of *Shadow Syndromes* (Ratey & Johnson, 1997), these people continue to be significantly impacted on a daily basis by their autistic tendencies. At that point, it can be difficult to tease out whether certain attributes result from one's personality or from the autism spectrum disorder. Perhaps it doesn't matter as long as the person with these issues receives the needed accommodations and understanding.

While one shouldn't blindly pigeon-hole children into any one of these categories, it appears to me that most children with autism fall mainly into one of these categories with possible small overlaps into the others.

Putting My Journey Through the Autism Spectrum in Context

MY PLACEMENT ON THE AUTISM SPECTRUM

A CLOSER LOOK AT MY PLACEMENT ON THE AUTISM SPECTRUM

Age	0	1.5	2.5	4	6	8	10	13	19
E V E N T S	Typical development Turning over at 8 days Rapid physical and motor development	Autism bomb hits Withdrawal from environment Tantrums	Putnam evaluation of atypical development, strong autistic tendencies & psychotic Early intervention from parents who refute recommendations for removal from home	Enter Putnam Condition improves to "neurotic" The wonderful world of watch motors Echolalia and return of speech Eating baby food	Kindergarten Social & academic difficulties Discovered making a mess of myself while eating BBQ chicken wings Loved cats, but dogs . . .	Special interests in astronomy and weather Teacher concerns about reading and math difficulties	Concern about dropping the letter "e" My friend says "he feels like a pizza" and I argue with him that he does not look like a pizza and probably does not feel like one either	Middle and high school Finally getting it together but still often in left field Discovering the band room Time to focus more on people and not their bicycles	College More friends Dating Others really do think differently Utopia!

Looking back on my life at age two and a half, as indicated by the large white dot in graphic on page 159, I place myself at that time in the moderate range of the autism spectrum. I was mute and had a limited awareness of my environment. Although these traits pointed me towards the severe end of the spectrum, my ability to be engaged via touch and the fact that my mother was able to reach me via imitation moved me towards the middle section of the graph. My ability to form a close bond with my mother at that time further ensconced me near the midpoint.

Stretching the right half of the autism spectrum diagram as seen on page 160 allows for a closer focus on my relationship to autism over time. The arrow depicts my movement through the spectrum. As previously stated, after first developing in a typical manner, at about 18 months of age I lost my verbal abilities and started to exhibit several autistic traits. By primary school, my verbal ability was just about on a par with that of the other children in my class. My special interests in astronomy, weather and other subjects began to appear in first grade when I was eight years old. My reading ability was better than my expressive language. I recognized many words in the printed form but not in the spoken. At this time I was at the lighter end of the autism spectrum.

I credit my movement through the autism spectrum to a fortunate confluence of the following: *Early Intervention*

1. *Early intervention from my parents.*

   Flying in the face of recommendations from the "professionals," my parents did the initial work by themselves. As it is easy to redirect the growth of a young sapling before it becomes a tree, the same can be said for a youngster with autism.

2. *The Putnam Children's Center.*

   Although less was known about working with children on the autism spectrum at that time than now, my nursery school teacher seemed to understand what the children in her classroom needed. She encouraged interaction between us and narrated our activities.

3. Maturation of my own nervous system and the ability to reflect on my own strengths and weaknesses.

My parents' openness about my relationship with the autism spectrum as early as age six allowed me to understand from early on that I had differences from most of my classmates. Thus, it permitted me to work on developing schemes for accommodations.

During my primary school days, the psychotherapy I was undergoing for "emotional disturbances" began to have some benefit as I was verbal enough to engage in discussions with the counselor. As a result, it was determined that my emotional difficulties stemmed from being on the autism spectrum.

The waning days of high school is when I began to edge beyond the autism spectrum. Although by my freshman year in college I probably would not have been diagnosed with Asperger Syndrome, residuals of the disorder still remained. While I was enthralled with the idea that I could be accepted for who I was at the university, these residuals continued to haunt me in dating and being able to build a workable structure out of the less-structured courses. The need for structure is what got me in trouble with the physics of music, while the ability to latch onto a structured approach was a boon when I took a course in systems analysis and design. These residuals continued to manifest themselves as difficulties with subtle social situations such as office politics at the accounting firm and the music position at the college. Facial recognition of students remains a challenge to me in college when I teach.

Getting haircuts and eating cherry tomatoes that burst in my mouth no longer present a sensory overload. Whereas the social implications of giving up my seat to an older gentleman on the bus used to be a complete mystery to me, I now comprehend why this is necessary. I still lack some of the social graces and understanding that seem to come so naturally to most people. However, I am aware that these social rules exist. By working with mentors such as the dean of business of the school where I taught, along with creating algorithms for social situations, I am working at getting better at them. In other words, by talking with this man I was able to script out how to respond to different political scenarios that *social stories* might crop up at the school.

The most important breakthrough occurred when my mother led me back to the castle of the autism spectrum with *Thinking in Pictures* by Temple Grandin. It was at this time I realized that the autism spectrum was not "all done." It is not something of the deep, dark, and buried past but instead is very much in the present. I came to understand that the autism spectrum is, and always will be, a part of me. All I can do is learn better how to work *with*, rather than against, the traits and characteristics of this differently ordered way of being. Hopefully, as I travel this path I can help others develop a better understanding of their personal existence on the autism spectrum. One example of working with, rather than against, the autism spectrum is to realize how many people with autism, including myself, process social interaction.

Approximating an Intuitive Sense of Social Interaction

Creating algorithms for social interactions helps greatly in getting along in the non-spectrum[15] world. Social algorithms can be constructed with others or, depending on the situation, by the person on the autism spectrum himself. Whereas most people learn social rules by observation, those on the autism spectrum often need to acquire them

---

[15] I have Roger Meyer to thank for coming up with an alternate way of designating people who are not on the autism spectrum without using the slightly derogatory "neurotypical" label.

cognitively. It feels similar to running Windows PC emulation software on a Macintosh. Although it usually works very well, performance suffers in terms of speed, smoothness, and other minor differences.

Social skills of person not on the autism spectrum

Viewing the non-spectrum person's set of social interaction skills as a circle, it is as if people on the autism spectrum start out with a square.

Social skills of person on the autism spectrum

For each algorithm built, two sides are added to the polygon to represent each situation where a person's repertoire of social interaction enables the person to take on the other person's point of view.

Social skills of person on the autism spectrum after appropriate intervention

The increasing number of sides makes it more and more difficult to calculate the area of this polygon, whereas figuring out the area of a circle remains relatively easy. As social interaction skills improve, the sides continue to increase in number.

Social skills of person on the autism spectrum after further appropriate intervention

Even though the polygon becomes ever more difficult to differentiate from a true circle, a perfectly round shape is never quite achieved. This means that people on the autism spectrum often need to learn social interactions cognitively rather than by observation. While it may be possible to approximate intuitive social interaction skills, some areas can remain rough just as a multisided wheel of a car will give a rougher ride than one that is a perfect circle.[16]

As I first heard discussed by my good friend and colleague Jean-Paul Bovee,[17] it is interesting to note that my own theory of mind difficulties more commonly occur when I interact with non-spectrum people but rarely when relating to others on the autism spectrum. Additionally, as mentioned by Jean-Paul Bovee, the theory of mind issue cuts both ways. Inasmuch as people on the autism spectrum need to understand and interact in a largely non-spectrum world, people who are not on the autism spectrum need to work on understanding those who are on the spectrum.

Overcoming the Wall

There continues to be many challenges as I travel on life's fascinating journey. Everyone has barriers to overcome that are special to each person. Whether they are intrinsically or extrinsically based, they are all very real. While the goals and milestones that lie beyond the wall are important, it is what is learned and shared with others that matters.

This is a period of great transition for me with the twin challenges of completing a doctoral degree in order to remain a college professor and reformatting my life plans for employment. The system I had set up for myself – a career as a professor of music with a doctorate – was interrupted. From the confusion and uncertainty that went along with this interrupted system must come an expansion of my life into new and uncharted areas. Like the nonverbal child with autism who communicates "down" for

---

[16] I am indebted to Philip Schwarz for enlightening me to and allowing me to use this metaphor involving polygons and emulation software (personal communication, February 4, 2001).

[17] I am indebted to Jean-Paul Bovee for first making me aware of this concept and for our further discussions about this subject.

the first time as I stop him from going down a slide just after he sits down and hitches forward, I too must expand my vocabulary of experiencing life as the changes come. I don't know where all this will lead but I do believe that the journey will be at least as rewarding as meeting the twin goals of obtaining the doctorate and meaningful employment.

Along with my interests in special education, computers and music, I am strongly drawn towards studying different learning styles and how such knowledge can be applied to teaching students at the college level. In particular, I am interested in students with mild, but disruptive, learning disabilities, especially those at the higher-functioning end of autism and Asperger Syndrome.

As my work with people of all abilities and the study of how to teach them continue along with the self-examination involved in writing this book, I have come in ever closer contact with my own learning style. Having worked through the challenges of an autism spectrum disorder enables me to use my life experiences to empathize with and help students in higher education with diffi-culties like mine.

My fascination with learning styles has been with me for as long as I can remember. For example, in grade school I often thought of alternative ways of presenting the lessons. In college, my inter-est in learning styles and various teaching methods was piqued when I took a course entitled Models of Teaching during my doc-toral work at Boston University. As we studied different learning styles and methods of teaching, I found that I intuitively knew some of these ideas and now was able to put a name to them. The theories and applications turned out to be an exciting new world to explore as I taught a diverse set of students in various schools in the Greater Boston area.

From the course on Models of Teaching, I realized that I need-ed to develop a strong structure on which to base my learning. Using this need for structure, I can build a framework that allows me to expand my knowledge base and experiences. Whether it is

Visual organization

the study of music theory or the preparation of a plan of action for a project, making a graphical representation of the material permits me to create order out of the swarm of ideas floating around in my head. I have seen a strong parallel of the need for structure with children on the autism spectrum, which involves establishing a system of functional behaviors and then working to expand this system. My graduate studies in music, along with my experiences with people of diverse ages and abilities on the autism spectrum, have also served to broaden my teaching repertoire.

My teaching experiences have taught me that there are some universal guidelines that must be adhered to for learning at all levels. One of these is the importance of transitions. This was driven home to me dramatically when I unexpectedly entered a room full of children diagnosed as having autism spectrum disorder at the Language and Cognitive Development Center and one of the children suddenly had a tantrum. I had to leave the room while the child was prepared for my arrival. After this preparation had been carried out, I could enter the room without the student making a fuss.

Transitions at the college level are far subtler, yet just as critical. The student, no matter what age or ability, has to be able to detect when there is a change in task or subject. Too often, when transitions are ineffectively framed, students are confused by the presentation of the lesson.

A developmental computer class of mine included two students who were friends and had opposite learning styles. One of them was extremely visually oriented – concepts and ideas had to be presented graphically with pictures. As most of my own knowledge is stored graphically, it was easy to convert the subject matter into a pictorial format that she could understand. As graphically oriented as she was, her friend's informational approach was totally textually and sequentially based. Everything needed to be spelled out in written form in a step-by-step manner. Not only was she

unable to learn from pictures, graphical presentations confused her. In fact, she was so text-oriented that she was
unable to keep a mental map of where the classroom was in
relation to the exits in order to leave the building. She
depended on someone else to guide her about the school.
Most important was the fact that these two women had very
different ways of processing information. My goal in such
extreme situations is to teach to the student's preferred
learning style while striving to expand her capabilities to
receive information in a different format.

I recently had the opportunity to put my ideas into practice
with a young man who is diagnosed with high-functioning
autism, who had enrolled in a computer course I taught. He
was intelligent and facile on the computer. However, he
had some learning-style and social issues that needed to
be accommodated in order that he could learn both the
subject material and proper classroom interaction. For
example, one day when I projected an outline of the day's
topics that spelled "computer" as "komputer," this student
blurted out loudly, "Computer is not spelled with a 'k'!"
Also, he ignored in-class assignments in favor of surfing the
Internet. It is important to realize that this student was not
acting defiant or lazy.

Seeing this incorrect spelling was simply unbearable to this
student's need for order. A simple expression of thanks on
my part and a correction of the spelling satisfied him at the
moment of the outburst. Afterwards, upon being instructed
to raise his hand before talking in class, his observations of
typographical errors occurred at more appropriate times.
He needed the structure of being told specifically, in a step-
by-step manner, the requirements of the class projects in
order to complete them. With surfing the Internet to look

forward to, he often finished the daily assignments in about a quarter of the time it took the rest of the class.

A student with attention deficit disorder was finding it impossible to familiarize himself with the connections and wiring of the audio equipment that was used in an electronic music class I taught. I suggested that he draw a map representing each module, its function, and how the pieces were connected to other modules. After spending an afternoon examining the individual devices, functions, and their connections, and representing all of it in pictorial form, he had a solid understanding of the entire electronic music studio. By accommodating his preferred visual-kinesthetic learning style, he was able to gain a deeper understanding of how the equipment functioned in the lab. Afterwards, I asked him to write a one-paragraph summary of what each module did in the studio. As a result of the success with this student, I have included mapping out the electronic music studio as one of the assignments for the electronic music course.

The borderline between accommodation of different learning styles and good teaching practice is very fuzzy. I believe that being aware of different learning styles and methods is a subset of the skills needed to be an effective teacher.

While I work well with people on the autism spectrum, I feel it is important to remain involved with the entire population of those with mild learning disabilities. Researching different learning and instructional methods along with the ever-increasing reliance on computer technology is important to me. I look forward to sharing my work experience with fellow students, teachers, and colleagues to assist all who are involved in creating a richer educational experience. In brief, my goal in becoming more involved in the study and practice of learning and teaching styles is to become a more effective educator.

I have revisited the Castle. The trip back to this edifice meant retracing my steps over the moat with its swarming reptiles, revisiting the guards at every turn, finding the secret stairway to the highest tower and locating that special key to unlock the room I occupied as a youngster. It is now time to move on; not to forget the past but to draw on it as a resource from which to help others and myself. My stay in the Castle as I wrote this book was both painful and exhilarating and it taught me much.

CHAPTER FOURTEEN

Cleared for Takeoff

After the first edition of *Beyond the Wall* was published, Arnold Miller inquired if I would like to meet someone who, like me, had attended the James Jackson Putnam Children's Center. This was the school where staff upon my original diagnosis suggested that separation from my family would be best for all. The person Arnold wanted me to meet had gone through the Putnam School a few years before me, so there was no way I could have seen him during my time there. Arnold informed me that this person, an airline pilot, was struggling with what may be some of the lighter traits of the autism spectrum. Since airplanes and flying was a special interest of mine as a child, I eagerly agreed to meet with him.

After some e-mail communications and phone calls, we decided to meet at a local restaurant for lunch. We had a good time talking about airplanes, Asperger Syndrome, and the possibility of him having this condition. While he remains unsure of whether he has Asperger Syndrome, he considers it a strong possibility. In keeping with our talk of airplanes, as I mounted my bicycle to ride home, I asked him, "Cleared for takeoff?" to which he responded without missing a beat, "Proceed at will." The two of us meet regularly, enjoy our mutual special interest in airplanes, and discuss the ramifications of being on the autism spectrum.

Commencement

Commencement is not the end ... just the beginning. While the completion of *Beyond the Wall* was a culmination of a lot of hard work, it was the beginning of ever-deeper involvement in several areas pertaining to the autism spectrum. My involvement has been and remains at all levels of autism. However, my focus now leans towards the high-functioning and Asperger end of the autism spectrum. Areas of involvement include working with people on the spectrum as discussed earlier, presentations, advocacy, and political involvement by serving on the boards of regional and national organizations.

Presentations

This "taking off" of my involvement with autism spectrum-related issues started with my attendance and presentation of workshops at the 2000 Autism Society of America (ASA) conference in Atlanta, Georgia. After becoming connected to a vast network of people on the autism spectrum, parents, and professionals, invitations to speak at conferences increased to such a point that I am often asked to present up to four or more times a month. At these events I continue to be impressed with all the people who are all working for the benefit of those on the autism spectrum.

In recent years there has been a steady increase in the public's awareness of the issues surrounding autism. When I started presenting, some of the more common questions involved when I was toilet trained and when I started to speak. The questions of today tend to center more on accommodations at school and how people can better interact with those having autism, as well as sensory variances that go along with the autism spectrum. Finally, there is a much greater presence of people on the autism spectrum both in the audience and among presenters.

In addition to exchanging knowledge about autism, these conferences are great places for people on the spectrum to meet and form, as well as strengthen, their ties to the community of those with autism. I have seen several first-time conference attendees who are on the spectrum come to the wonderful realization that they are not alone – that there are many others like them. These conferences can greatly help build community and self-esteem for people with autism.

Advocacy

Advocacy is realizing what a person needs in order to maximize his or her functioning in life and knowing how to arrange the environment or obtain the necessary accommodations to do so. Or put another way, it is being literate about a person's needs. Advocacy can be done at all levels, ranging from helping an individual to working on an international level to benefit people on the autism spectrum around the world. The road to advocacy includes discussions of disclosure, special interests, learning styles, learning accommodations, and even relationships.

Advocating for oneself can be particularly challenging because many people on the autism spectrum are unaware of exactly what they need in order to function at maximum capacity and/or fail to realize that changes can be made. In recent years, much effort has been placed on teaching adults with Asperger Syndrome the tools of self-advocacy. That is great; however, I feel that learning to advocate for oneself is a lifelong process that should start the moment it is known that a person has an autism spectrum disorder.

Advocacy in Education as Training for Advocacy in Life

Given that the public schools are charged with enabling the nation's youth to lead fulfilling and productive lives, it only makes sense to include self-advocacy as part of that education for all students with disabilities. At this point most education professionals start thinking about teaching self-advocacy to students at age 14, as this is when transition planning for life after high school graduation is mandated in the Individualized Education Plan (IEP). However, this is too late. As much as possible, students should be involved in developing and leading their own IEP process because doing so will teach them to manage their own self-advocacy process. As mentioned in *Student-Led IEPs* (McGahee, Mason, Wallace, & Jones, 2001), given the great variance of student ability, there is a wide range of options. Some students may just be able to state or read part of their plan for the future to the IEP team, others may go on to explain their disability, describe the need for accommodations, share their strengths and challenges (present levels of performance), and talk about plans for the future. The eventual goal is a student-led IEP meeting (under the watchful eyes of the IEP team).

The self-initiated IEP is a great way to do this. Information about teaching students to manage their own IEPs can be downloaded from the National Information Center for Children and Youth with Disabilities (NICHCY) website publication, *A Student's Guide to the IEP* (McGahee-Kovac, 2002), and the accompanying Technical Assistance Guide, *Helping Students Develop Their Own IEP* (NICHCY, 2002). Self-advocacy is vital because of the paradigm shift from being advocated for through the IEP to advocating for oneself. Many young adults on the spectrum are forced to learn the realities of self-advocacy after graduation from public schools and entering the community, workforce, or higher education. In addition to knowing what her needs are, when a student's self-advocacy skills are built through the self-initiated IEP process, she will have a greater understanding of how to obtain the required accommodations to meet her needs.

The ramifications from failing to acquire sufficient self-advocacy skills can be very debilitating. For example, at the higher education level, students in this unfortunate position often think that special education is "all done" and now want to "be just like everyone else," entering college unaware of their needs and/or refusing to meet with the Student Support Office. However, variances in learning styles remain with the person, and often around the middle of the semester difficulties in coursework mount and the student realizes that he needs help. Obtaining such assistance at that late stage presents many challenges, ranging from finding the appropriate office in the college or university to preparing the necessary documentation and obtaining proper accommodations.

Just as it is easier to correct errors and edit another person's writing than one's own, it is often easier to advocate for another person. Often people with Asperger Syndrome serve as highly effective advocates for others as they have first-hand experiences living the challenges we live with every day.

Political Involvement

During my travels around the country presenting on autism spectrum disorders, I was encouraged to run for the board of directors of the Autism Society of America. At first I was opposed, because I felt it was a political thing to do. I do not consider myself a political person. In fact, I have always avoided politics because it seemed to require too much higher-order level theory of mind. In other words, in addition to needing to know what others were thinking through nonverbal channels of communication, politics appeared to require the ability to realize when someone was verbally telling you one thing but really intending something entirely different, all of which is difficult for many on the autism spectrum to detect. Therefore, politics to me had always been a confusing swarm of words that either had different meanings from their face value or meant nothing at all.

After much consideration and gentle nudging and support from friends such as Nancy Cale of Unlocking Autism and Jerry Silbert, I decided to run. When Jerry Newport, a staunch advocate and activist on autism-related issues, found out I was running after all, he personified the generous, logical nature of many people with Asperger Syndrome by immediately telling me that he too was running and suggesting we support each other. We trusted each other and felt that while it would be best if both of us won seats, one of us would be sufficient as we communicated with each other enough to know how we felt on certain issues. Not surprisingly, therefore, when I won the election, Jerry was quick to congratulate me and offer his support. I look to Jerry as a sort of "big brother" in the Asperger community.

Working with others in effecting real change for people on the autism spectrum is very satisfying. One of the high points of my experiences in this area was when I was invited to testify on the state of autism-related issues to the chair of Governmental Reform, Dan Burton, in April 2002. Ever since his grandchild was diagnosed with autism, Mr. Burton has been a strong advocate for proper allocation of resources for autism-related issues. Since Lee Grossman, president of the Autism Society of America, was also selected to testify, we spent many late-night hours working closely to ensure that our presentations complemented each other. With only a couple of weeks to prepare for such a momentous task with such grave responsibility, we questioned whether we were up to the task. There was so much to say and so little time to prepare and then actually say it ... to the Congressional Reform Committee of the United States of America.

Part of my presentation to this committee included the desperate need for services. The term "services" is to be approached with great caution because it may imply that those on the autism spectrum are looking for a hand-out from society. While it is true that individuals with autism may need additional assistance from the community at large, it is important that these services result in helping those with autism lead as fulfilling and productive lives as possible. What is really needed is a hand-up.

A Desperate Need for a Hand-Up – Not a Hand-Out

We desperately need more educational research. While there is some literature that supports best practice for children and youth with moderate to severe autism spectrum disorders, the same cannot be said for individuals with high-functioning autism and Asperger Syndrome. As a result, potentially thousands of individuals are exposed to educational interventions that are not validated or appropriate for them or, perhaps even more tragic, not exposed to interventions at all because the educational community does not know what to do. Due to the vast diversity in people with autism, there is no one methodological approach that suits all children. Rigorous academic research into the effects of comparative methodologies is needed because interventions must be tailored to fit a person's particular academic, cognitive, developmental, behavioral, social, sensory, and other needs. *goals*

More effort also needs to be placed on teacher training and educational research so that educators of children and youth with autism spectrum disorders understand the condition and can translate research into practice as well as document child progress through assessment. The implications of this lack of resources are enormous, resulting in a large cohort of children and adults who do not receive vitally needed early intervention and assistance to successfully navigate their environment.

According to data from the University of California Davis Health Systems, the conservative cost of a lifetime of care (including only transportation, day services, and residential care) for every person with severe autism in California's developmental services system is about $85,000 a year

(University of California Regents, 2000). This calculates to a staggering almost 6 million dollars over the average life-span. When multiplied by the as many as 1,500,000 individuals with autism in the United States (Autism Society of America, 2002), the figure balloons into the quadrillions. Even so, this raw dollar amount does not even begin to express the opportunity cost of lost wages and other contributions to society such as charitable work and playing in musical ensembles. All people on the autism spectrum need appropriate and timely intervention in order to be given the same chance that only a select few individuals have had due to luck, family, education and other circumstances to succeed in life.

If the Center for Disease Control estimates that one out of 250 kids have autism right now, they need to consider that in 10-15 years one out of 250 adults will have autism, and then what will we do? Funds devoted to research and early intervention now will pay huge dividends later.

Some ways to increase resources include immediate and abundant funding for research, education, and fellowships to expand the number of skilled medical doctors, teachers, and other professionals working with people on the autism spectrum. Also, recognizing autism as a medical neurobiological, as opposed to a psychiatric, condition as it relates to insurance payments will eliminate mental health coverage policy constraints. In addition, standardizing payments for recognized methods of interventions across the country is vital because there is no one particular approach that satisfies the needs of all children with autism spectrum disorders. Some sound approaches include but are not limited to the Miller Method (Miller & Eller-Miller, 1989; Miller, 2000); Floortime (Greenspan & Wieder, 1998); Daily Life Therapy from the Higashi School (Kitihara, 1983); Treatment and Education of Autistic and Related Communication Handicapped

Children (TEACCH) (Cohen, 2002; Schopler, Reichler, & Lansing, 1980); and applied behavioral analysis (ABA) as developed by Ivar Lovaas (Lovaas, Ackerman, Alexander, Firestone, Perkins, & Young, 1981; Lovaas, 1987, 2002; Lovaas & Smith, 1989).

As board president of the Asperger's Association of New England and board member of several other autism spectrum-related organizations, I unfortunately see most adults on the autism spectrum functioning way below their potential in many areas such as community involvement, employment, relationships, housing, and education. In addition, there is a large number of adults who want to access universities but need support in academics, housing, and relationships in order to be successful.

In most areas of the United States, persons with high-functioning autism and Asperger Syndrome fall in the cracks between governmental agencies. For example, in Massachusetts they are not served by the Department of Mental Retardation because their IQ exceeds the 70-point threshold required to be considered as having mental retardation, and the Department of Mental Health refuses to assist because it does not consider high-functioning autism and Asperger Syndrome to be mental disorders. Perhaps a new governmental agency that works with pervasive developmental disorders (which includes autism and Asperger Syndrome) would be much more helpful, as some states have already done.

Some additional recommendation that I made to Dan Burton's Committee on Governmental Reform included working with organizations such as the Autism Society of America by supporting their funding requests and in developing legislation regarding the autism spectrum as well as implementation of documents such as the National Research Council's "Educating Children with Autism" report recommendations.

While many sound interventions and treatments for autism are available, some families have to wait for years before receiving desperately needed early intervention services. Organizations like the National Institute of Health need to work with organizations such as the Autism Society of America in developing national policy for people within the autism community so that *all* those having autism have a fair shot at leading fulfilling, productive, and independent lives to the extent of their capacities. My complete testimony is on my website at www.autismasperger.info.

What's Next for Me?

I see continued involvement with my peers, educators, and others in pursuit of improving the life chances of people on the autism spectrum. Upon finishing my doctorate in special education I will seek a faculty position in higher education, combining my interests in teaching future educators how to work with people having special needs and my research into the best practices of teaching those on the spectrum how to successfully navigate in the environment.

The future for people on the autism spectrum looks promising but much remains to be done. With increased prevalence and awareness, perhaps the cause of autism can follow in the footsteps of other conditions. It was not long ago that a terrible stigma was attached to attention deficit disorder and acquired immunity deficiency. However, with well-planned organizations providing information to the public, people have become more accepting of people with these conditions. Hopefully, the condition of autism spectrum disorders is moving in the same direction. For example, it is now common for people in the United States to recognize the word "autism" (although still less so "Asperger Syndrome"). More now realize that autism is not necessarily a life sentence of isolation and withdrawal from society but a collection of some significant strengths as well as challenges to surmount.

A Challenge to the
Autism Spectrum Community

Those of us in the autism spectrum community were inducted in one of several ways. One cohort consists of those whose child or the child of someone close has autism. Another group includes educators ranging from preschool to college as well as aides and educational administrators. Yet another collection of people consists of researchers and scientists looking for ways to help those on the spectrum better interact within our environment.

Finally, and most important, are the individuals who have autism themselves. We are a diverse group with many different viewpoints and agendas. However, I think everyone in the autism spectrum community has the common goal of doing what is right for people with autism. As suggested by Dan Burton's Committee for Governmental Reform, the autism community wields a lot of power and ability to do well for those with autism. However, the Governmental Reform Committee likened the autism community to a "600-pound gorilla that is asleep at the wheel." In order to meet our needs, the committee stressed the importance of returning to them as a single unified entity with one voice.

We need to lay aside personal agendas and work together. Working together, as opposed to political factions and fiefdoms, is the way to empowerment that will enable us to do what's best for those with autism. Everyone will benefit as a result.

CHAPTER FIFTEEN

Epilogue and Charge of Responsibility

I am in the dissertation stage of my doctoral degree in special education at Boston University. The work is challenging and has stretched me in ways that I have at times thought unimaginable. While some of the work has required an enormous amount of restructuring of course materials, there are no major parts of my learning style that I have not been able to self-accommodate for.

As mentioned earlier, some of the first people to wash ashore on to the beach of increasing public understanding of life with autism were Donna Williams and Temple Grandin. The tide of knowledge continued to come in with others such as Thomas Mckean and Sean Barron. We are now at full neap tide with Edgar Schneider, Gunilla Gerland, Liane Willey, and myself. But there is much more to come. There are many others on and off the autism spectrum who will contribute to this ever-expanding and deepening web of experience and knowledge about this different way of being. In addition to helping those with autism and Asperger Syndrome, all people, of all abilities will benefit.

We have crested an era where people, some officially diagnosed and others not, who grew up during the dawning awareness of the autism spectrum as a disorder have told their stories. Much good work has been done by scientists and researchers on the causes of autism and Asperger Syndrome; yet no conclusive source or sources have been identified. We have dispelled the myth that autism has psychological causes while recognizing that there may be psychological issues that are secondary to this different order of being. Additionally, we have learned much about how to teach and be with people on the autism spectrum. Finally, there has been a lot of progress towards changing the societal construct of people with autism.

It is these last two points that I and all who are on the autism spectrum who write, talk about and otherwise present about their lives must address. We are not here to function as "self-narrating zoo exhibits,"[18] but to increase mutual understanding among those with autism and society at large.

The responsibility to help current and future generations of children with autism and Asperger Syndrome develop their strengths in order to lead meaningful lives in our society belongs to all of us. This includes people on or near the spectrum, family members, teachers, and anyone who comes in contact with people with autism and Asperger Syndrome. The young children of today are the first generation to benefit from this large-scale availability of first-hand experience on the autism spectrum. This book represents my small contribution to this effort. These responsibilities are heavy and serious. If this autobiography has engendered greater mutual understanding among society of life on and slightly to the right of the autism spectrum; if this work has assisted even one person in developing a more meaningful relationship with a person on the autism spectrum; if only one person with autism has been helped – then I have achieved my goal of developing more understanding and building bridges to a better tomorrow.

---

[18] This term was coined by Jim Sinclair, co-founder, with Donna Williams and Kathy Grant, of Autism Network International. "Self-narrating zoo exhibit" refers to when persons on the autism spectrum present about their life and a lack of equal status as whole human beings is found between the speaker and the audience. In this situation the term describes a limitation imposed by society so that such presentations merely provide raw data about interesting phenomena. (Personal communication, October 15, 2000, Jim Sinclair).

I have had the pleasure of combining knowledge from the work I do at the Language and Cognitive Development Center, my doctoral program in special education at Boston University, and personal experience to help those on the autism spectrum I work with. My overriding hope is that I am able to give back to those associated with the autism spectrum – whether they are on it themselves, or care for or live with a person with autism – as much as I have received from these wonderful and brave people.

Appendix A
An Interview with Daniel Rosenn, M.D.

As part of this "research project" on my life, Dr. Rosenn was one of many people I talked with in order to help make sense of my relation to the lighter end of the autism spectrum and Asperger Syndrome. Dr. Daniel Rosenn is a psychiatrist, who specializes in working with children and young adults with high-functioning autism and Asperger Syndrome. Below are some of the things we discussed concerning this autobiography.

DR. ROSENN   I was fascinated to read the book because it gives someone like myself, who plays and talks with many people on the autistic spectrum, a better chance of learning what they're feeling. As you speak about your experiences as a child, it's like breaking open a fortune cookie or unlocking a code: "This is what I was feeling; it was a coldness of the bar on the swing set that made me hit my head on the patio. It wasn't Martin at all, it was that cold bar that made me do this." It confirms for me that there is an understandable basis for autistic behavior. And even though I'm not always sure of what it is, I appreciate the chance to go back into your childhood and sort through your reactions and behaviors to get the motivations cleared for us.

STEPHEN   Do most people with Asperger Syndrome have difficulty with feelings? Add to that question, "How do you account for the fact that I'm able to experience profound feelings with the Arnold Schoenberg cantata as depicted in this book?"

DR. ROSENN I found that passage very, very moving. It's as if a piece of you came alive in a new way and flooded you with feelings. I think what struck me as particularly moving in your experience of the cantata was that the music itself unlocked for you this surge of emotions. With "neurotypical" people, these feelings seem more accessible and spontaneous. Physical beauty, style of dress, the way other people move and look release surges of feelings, sometimes inappropriate and wonderfully motivating in terms of pushing for a connection. So people talk poetically about a woman being a symphony of grace whereas you were unlocked by the actual sound properties and the associations of the music you were hearing. How did that work for you? When you think about it, can you tell me how it happened?

STEPHEN Well, it's my belief that music works better than words in communication for people on the autism spectrum because music lights up or accesses a different part of the brain than does oral communication. As far as communication is concerned, I feel that for some people at the more severe end of the spectrum, music can be a way to communicate. And for people who are at the higher end, music can serve as a carrier signal to help organize and decode the meaning of words and language. I think that's what happened to me. I had read the text that goes along with the cantata, and the text itself is very graphic. It is fairly moving but the addition of music provides another dimension with which to experience affect. When I work with children, music helps a lot, and it's a great tool to help them organize their being, their thoughts, and the activities they have to do. For example, I've noticed that people who are most successful in working with these children, at any level, talk musically. For example, they'll say "Sit down," descending a minor third. That melody, I believe, helps to communicate to the child. They also speak rather rhythmically, and rhythm helps too.

DR. ROSENN I think what's so interesting about you, and I don't know when this started, is that you have had strong intellectual curiosity. I can see it as you described yourself as a child, it was clearly there in taking apart clocks, which is common for kids on the spectrum. But I think your drive to know and to decipher and understand social complexities is quite rare. You are, as far as I can tell, not nearly as uncomfortable by what you don't know as others on the spectrum.

STEPHEN Yes, it's like I can observe them from afar or at a distance as opposed to kind of fusing and not being able to separate. How do you account for the fact that I'm able to empathize with the feelings of others?

DR. ROSENN Give me some examples of what you're talking about?

STEPHEN For example, when I write about the effects that the residuals of echolalia presenting themselves as echopraxia and echoemotica have on me, there was one time when I was talking to my mother on the phone and I just felt an overwhelming sense of blackness. Later on I called her back and asked if there was something wrong, and indeed there was. Sometimes I even feel there is a fusion with another person's feelings. When this happens I get a feeling, and I'm not sure where it comes from. I sort of have to examine it and ask myself, "Should I really be feeling this way or is it coming from somebody else?"

DR. ROSENN   Now I understand what you mean by "empathy." That's slightly different from what I think of as empathy although they are clearly related. I think that over the years, because some avenues of connection were cut off for you, other avenues of connection, of sensing sensation, became hypertrophied (or accentuated). And I think that as a result you learned very early on, particularly with your mother, to follow signals so sensitively that you couldn't break them down to see what they were. Many children do that but I think for you, your mother was a lifeline, a real emotional lifeline. Without her, you would be cut off from the world. And so it became incredibly important for you to be able to do this. You could tune in at these kinds of meta-communicating levels with her, particularly in the past. You've probably gotten less proficient at it lately I would suspect – it's less crucial to you now.

STEPHEN   Right, it is less crucial. I spend less time with my mother and more time with others such as my wife.

DR. ROSENN   Now empathy involves that, but it's a little different. With "empathy," as I understand the word, you remain who you are, but you feel some of the other person's feelings without losing your own perspective. You can move back and forth fluidly, almost simultaneously, between yourself and the other person. One uses a broader context than just facial signaling – this is the way that person must feel because this is the way I would feel if I were in that person's shoes.

It's that kind of transaction that is very, very hard for AS people even though it can be very intellectual. That often doesn't get put into words for "neurotypical" persons; they just sort of do it. And with AS people often the best they can do is to reason it out, "What would it feel like to me if I were doing this?" Because of theory of mind impairments, AS people perceive things so differently from others that what they would be feeling in a situation could be very different from what a "neurotypical" person would feel. A "neurotypical" person might be feeling, for example, romantic sadness or something like that, whereas people with AS might be feeling, "I have to get out of there; this is dangerous." This makes empathy very hard for them.

In some other examples that you alluded to about your wife, I think you do empathize in the ways that I was talking about. What it says to me is that people on the autistic spectrum strive to grow and connect. This tropism towards connection and reciprocity is like plants on a windowsill growing towards the light. People grow towards each other even on the autistic spectrum. You are an example of someone who continues to do it. I don't have the answer as to why you can do it, in particular, but I think for many people it goes back to earlier experiences with loving relationships in their childhood. This optimism probably goes back to your household, which I know had its troubles. But it sounds like your mother, despite all of her challenges, her pain and her misery at times, was incredibly committed and devoted. You came to believe that people could care. There was a kind of connection that would carry on in the midst of pain.

STEPHEN   Why do you suppose I have done as well as I have? Are there some special qualities that you feel have made my progress possible?

DR. ROSENN Well, for one thing, there is a quality of optimism about you. A feeling of patience and a kind of quiet hopefulness. Now, I don't know when that emerged or whether it was there when you were a child. I also think there is a quality of courage. You've put yourself out into the real world, which many similar people would not have. You went to a public elementary school without much support and lived through the early years of teasing and the pain that came from that. Many kids on the spectrum would have refused to go to school or would have become aggressive.

Some might say, well maybe that's passivity. I think you had this feeling that things could and would get better, and that's been really important. I also find you communicate a quality of respectfulness and reflectiveness. You're interested in thinking about things. You are an examiner. You're someone who's curious about the way the world works, and you've found a niche for yourself with other people who have that same quality. You're involved in a teaching and learning setting. Clearly, if you had chosen for your life's work to be an accountant or working at a brokerage firm, these qualities would probably not have been very adaptive for you. Because of your interests, and because of serendipity, your musical skills, and your intellectual skills, you gravitated to a safer place where your resources can flourish and you can take advantage of them.

And then the final factor, which I think is so remarkable, is that you have a wish to give back what's been given to you. You want to help other children and young adults with various kinds of challenges. You have been helping them make a go of it the way people helped you. I find something very spiritual in that. It's not just the symmetry, but there's something of a higher ethic, which I find really admirable.

STEPHEN   Thank you. In your judgment, did the fact that my wife is Chinese, from a different culture, help me in becoming involved and ultimately marrying her?

DR. ROSENN   Well, again, I don't know very much about this, except the little bit we talked about and what I've read in your book. But I suspect that in some ways the things that you've alluded to have been helpful. The fact that your wife was new to the country and new to the language must have helped. And not just the verbal part of the language, but especially the nonverbal. Being an immigrant, she probably was less sensitive to, or critical of, ways in which you communicated differently from the "neurotypical" American.

But I also think there must be something unique about your wife, not that she's Chinese, necessarily, though I'm sure that's very important. She had the courage, the inner resources, and the motivation to break into a new culture and country. She had the capacity to ask for and accept your help around music. There's a kind of receptivity in this that must have worked to your advantage. You found not only a woman from a different culture, but a woman with her own wishes to affiliate, her own wishes to connect in uncharted territory, and her own courage to do all of that. I don't know her personally, but I suspect there's more to this than just the fact that she didn't demand as many facial signals. I bet there's part of her personality that worked to your benefit. She must have noticed that you were helpful and kind. She probably didn't care that you were not like John Wayne or his Chinese counterpart. The things that, for better or for worse, often release affiliative urges in our culture weren't important to her. It sounds to me like what was important were more universal and authentic qualities like the fact that she experienced you as a good person, that you have interests that she admired, and that you can enjoy things that she can enjoy. Does that make sense?

STEPHEN   Yeah, it makes a lot of sense. Some of the things
             she's told me herself about qualities she's looking
             for in people don't match up with the "neurotyp-
             ical" Western or even Eastern culture, or at least
             the culture that I know. How do you think "neu-
             rologically" typical people perceive me?

DR. ROSENN   I can't speak for anyone but myself. To me, you
             come across as a bright, caring, thoughtful person.
             You come across as diffident and respectful. I don't
             think superficially you would stand out as being
             different. I think people would have to get to know
             you better to see some of your vulnerabilities that
             are related to the autistic spectrum. Many of the
             grownups I've seen with AS have more difficulties
             with tonal inflections and prosody than you do.[16]
             People they're talking to may not ever have heard
             of Asperger, but the hair goes up on the back of
             their necks because of, say, the robotic or formal
             tone of voice.

             Also, many grownups with Asperger have commu-
             nication problems that are much more serious.
             Their gaze patterns are different. It's not just the
             eye contact. Many "neurotypicals" do not make
             constant eye contact when they interact either.
             Their eyes glance away, then come back at a punc-
             tuation point in the sentence. It's usually not
             intense eye contact. Many of the AS people that I
             see as grownups have been taught to make eye con-
             tact but their gaze patterns are still peculiar and

---

[19] Having to do with the elements of pitch, melody, tempo and interplay that most people handle on an automatic basis when speaking to others. A person with Asperger Syndrome may speak at too high a pitch or not know the proper time to break into a conversation with others.

overly intense. You also seem less reactive to the sensory properties of the environment. I know sometimes you startle, but many of the people on the high-functioning part of the spectrum are much more at the mercy of their environment. I assume you react internally but you can go limp with it better than a lot of other people, and that's another good thing.

STEPHEN   When observing children diagnosed with AS on the spectrum, is there anything you do to predict who will do well and who will not do well? Are there any predictors?

DR. ROSENN   I wish I knew. I think we're more often wrong than right when we start predicting the long-term future. Anyone who makes these predictions is really on very thin ice. With kids who are under the age of five, I don't like to predict even two or three years ahead. Between the ages of three and six, it's truly incredible how people who are, for example, in the PDD-NOS part of the spectrum just rush headlong to the high-functioning part of the spectrum. They acquire language, their flapping and a lot of their self-stimulatory behaviors begin to diminish or vanish. They learn social skills. Many three-year-olds who you think are going to be quite autistic at the age of six have grown into AS.

Younger children who start out on the high-functioning end of the spectrum are very hard to predict in terms of adult life. What we think we do know are some things that help optimize adaptation. For example, if a child on the high-functioning part of the spectrum lives in an abusive home with a drunken father or a highly depressed mother who cannot properly care for her kids, clearly that's a bad predictor for the future. Similarly, if a kid on the high-functioning part of the spectrum is in a school where the kids are allowed to tease or hurt her, that's a bad predictor for the future. But if a child has had someone important such as a mentor or a coach, a teacher, rabbi, psychiatrist or older brother or a friend, it could be anyone, someone who takes a real interest and is committed to the child, that's a wonderful help. Early intervention is important.

STEPHEN   I know a lot of people who have that gift, including a friend of my sister who is four years older than I am and a friend that I've made through bicycling. I always got along much better with people who were older than with people my own age.

DR. ROSENN   What is important in adulthood is that you were able to search out mentors. There is something about you that makes it possible for them to connect with you and want to help you. Not all people with AS have it. Obviously, you're very bright and I don't even know how to measure your kind of brightness. There are people with AS with very, very high IQs who don't have the things that we're talking about and have not done nearly as well in adult life. So intelligence is an important factor but probably not the most important. Children who have been blessed with a sunny nature and a warm disposition seem to do better than those who are more raw, vigilant, paranoid or suspicious. There are so many variables in the prognostic equation. Having good, loving parents helps a lot.

STEPHEN   What do you feel can be done for people with AS to maximize their development? Are there any specific things that you can suggest to people of different ages such as toddler, elementary, middle, high school, college and beyond?

DR. ROSENN   Thankfully, more and more has been written about the needs of these children. Temple Grandin's and Tony Attwood's books are examples. Many of the interventions that are used for nonverbal learning disabilities that Byron Rourke writes about are appropriate for AS, as are many interventions that are used for children with ADHD. But I think that no matter what the strategies are, the schools need a better understanding of what the social and neurocognitive deficits of these children are. Otherwise, they too often just blame them for their symptoms and take a moralistic and critical posture. I've seen schools where they know abstractly how to teach kids with AS, but their inability to understand empathically what the world is like for a child with AS gets in the way of their being good teachers.

Now, it's not because these teachers are bad people. It's not because they're uncaring, but to understand a child with AS requires a paradigmatical leap that is often counterintuitive. The hard part is to try to get them to understand what it's like on the inside for children with AS. That's why your book is so important. Your speaking engagements and the videotapes you've made are so important because people like you can explain what it was like for you as a child. You make it easier for people like me who are also trying to do this. That's another reason why your book is so powerful and so important.

Appendix B
Getting Ready for College[20]

The format and content of this section was developed and laid out by Dania Jekel and Stephanie Loo of the Asperger's Association of New England as a guide for helping individuals with Asperger Syndrome achieve success in the college experience. I have added some of my own thoughts and experiences along the way.

While I see many students with Asperger Syndrome doing well in college, a good number encounter serious challenges. The following, garnered from students, parents, and staff from the Asperger's Association of New England, suggests steps that can be taken to maximize the chances of success in college and use the college years to create a foundation for a satisfying, independent life after graduation.

Going away to college poses multiple challenges for every student, not just those with AS. For example, most college students are expected to:

- work more independently and take on more sophisticated, in-depth, or complex intellectual challenges.
- learn the rules of a new social environment. For example, a college freshman will face the challenges of meeting a lot of new people, making new friends, and participating in new social activities.

---

[20] I am indebted to Dania Jekel, executive director, and Stephanie Loo, staff associate, of the Asperger's Association of New England for granting me permission to include their work as the primary basis for this section.

- live more independently and rely less on their parents for practical help with things like laundry, meals, and personal finances.
- begin thinking about a career and making plans for life after graduation.

It is important to plan ahead to ensure that a person with Asperger Syndrome has the best chance of meeting the major challenges listed above and therefore benefit from and enjoy the college years. Among the many issues students and their families need to think about, we will look more closely at the following four:

1. Pick a college that is a good match, both academically and socially.
2. Submit proof to the college Disabilities Office of one's AS in order to obtain helpful supports and accommodations.
3. Establish a support network of people on and off campus who can help in key areas such as academics, living arrangements, and social issues.
4. Start early with career exploration and planning.

Pick a College That Is a Good Match

When researching potential colleges, look for institutions that meet most or all of the criteria in the list below. Most of the information can be found on college websites, in catalogues and guidebooks that evaluate and compare colleges, as well as by talking to the high school guidance counselor. Students currently in college are an additional resource.

Later, upon visiting or interviewing at colleges of interest, make observations and ask questions to verify that the college does in fact have the desired characteristics and services.

The following characteristics are helpful for most students with AS:

1. The college has a relatively small student body. Students are more likely to get the attention and assistance they need to do their best at a smaller school than at a large, impersonal university.

   > Acceptance into a major course of study such as music education, for example, in a small department can reduce the depersonalizing effect a large school can otherwise have. Part of the reason why I was successful in both the University of Massachusetts and at Boston University was that I was enrolled in small departments that ameliorated the effect of these schools' very large enrollments of over 25,000 students.

2. The college has good classes, professors, and programs in the student's area of strongest interest or talent.

3. The college offers some flexibility in terms of how students fulfill requirements or will consider waiving some requirements.

4. The college has a strong Disability Resource Center or Office of Disability Services, staffed by people who are familiar with and knowledgeable about Asperger Syndrome. Sometimes this office is referred to as the Office of Student Support or by other names. The Disability Office may include a learning/tutoring center where students can get help with organizing their work or extra help if needed in content-specific areas. They may also offer peer support groups or a one-on-one peer-mentoring program.

5. The college accepts students who live off campus or at home, and commute to campus.

6. The college has good systems in place for conflict resolution or problem solving. For example, a student accused of a disciplinary infraction can have an advocate attend hearings with him/her; decisions are made by experienced college personnel, rather than by committees of undergraduate students.

7. The college has the staff and systems in place to monitor the progress and well-being of individual students such as automatic notification of the student, advisor, and other key persons if a student seems to be falling behind in a class well before the end of the semester.
8. If the student agrees to it, the college accepts the value of parental involvement, and communicates well with parents. This is not very common.
9. The college has a diverse student body and a positive attitude toward individual differences. An example might be an art school or a school with a stated philosophy and reputation for valuing diversity and creativity.
10. The college offers good career services both during college and after graduation. Internship opportunities are available to help students prepare for work after graduation.
11. The college has clubs in the student's interest areas.
12. The college is located not too far from home.

For some students, it makes sense to break the challenge of completing a college degree up into smaller steps that can be tackled one by one, rather than all at once. One option is living at home while attending a nearby community college for one or two years and then transfer to a four-year institution, either continuing to live at home or moving into a dorm. Once the academic demands of college have been met, it may be easier to tackle the social, career preparation, and independent living challenges.

Be realistic. Colleges are educational, not rehabilitative institutions.

Disclosure, Accommodations, and Supports on Campus

"Disclosure" means telling key people that the student has Asperger Syndrome and explaining how it may get in the way of academic or social success. If certain supports are needed in order to graduate, then disclosure during the application process is strongly recommended. A college that is willing to admit a student on the autism spectrum is likely to offer an accepting atmosphere and the necessary supports and accommodations.

An effective approach to disclosure might include giving the college personnel an information packet like the one developed by the Asperger's Association of New England at www.aane.org, from which this section was closely derived. Another method of disclosure is to write one's own experiences as a person with Asperger Syndrome in the personal essay required on the college application form.

Since Asperger Syndrome is a legally recognized disability under the Americans with Disabilities Act, a person with this condition is entitled to appropriate supports and accommodations required to succeed in college. In order to obtain such supports and accommodations, the disclosure of Asperger Syndrome must be accompanied with recent written proof of the diagnosis from a qualified professional with recommendations for accommodations written in a style that is easy for the college to implement. (The Office of Disabilities often does not have expertise in Asperger Syndrome.) In almost all situations, having all the necessary documentation in order is mandatory before getting assistance from the Office of Disabilities. Coming to the Office of Disabilities prepared before classes start is much better than waiting until after classes start and offering Asperger Syndrome as an excuse or explanation later on, after problems have occurred.

Once the Disabilities Office staff receive *written permission* to disclose material about a student, they will be able to let that student's professors know what supports and accommodations are needed. Examples include time extensions to complete required research papers, extra time or quiet rooms for completing written exams, or permission to use a computer in an exam.

The liaison or case manager in the Disabilities Office will also be able to contact other college personnel who need to understand a student's situation, such as residence directors and assistants, security and judicial affairs officers. He or she might be able to secure a single room in the dorm – by far the best choice for most students with AS. (A student wanting a single room should communicate this to the Disabilities Office as far in advance as possible.)

Many college disability offices offer special orientation sessions for students before the semester begins. A good orientation covers all the specifics of the written and unwritten rules of college life. This chance to become familiar with the campus, the people, and the rules can give a valuable head start on college success. Some students attend a summer course on campus between the end of high school and the beginning of freshman year in order to have plenty of time to get used to the campus.

From the very beginning, students with Asperger Syndrome should meet with their academic advisors and liaison to decide if any of the academic requirements are likely to be unduly burdensome. If so, an *early* request for accommodation or waiver for those requirements should be submitted. For example, if math or foreign languages pose special challenges due to having AS, the student could negotiate for accommodations, make substitutions, or in some cases get those requirements dropped. The less the academic requirements need to be modified, the easier it will be to convince the Office of Disabilities to honor one's request.

Some students with AS find that their best strategy is to take fewer courses each semester and make up the credits by taking summer courses and/or by going to college for one or more extra years. Find out before enrolling if the college permits students to use this strategy, and if there is a lower fee each semester for students taking fewer courses.

Establish a Support Network

Set up a system of supports *before* starting college. Having good systems in place works *much* better than waiting for a problem to arise and then scrambling for a solution. In fact, it may make the critical difference between success and failure.

The person with Asperger Syndrome should have at least one person at the school (probably a Disabilities Office staff person or a psychologist) to act as an overall liaison. Whatever the person's official title, he or she should be someone who both understands Asperger Syndrome and knows all the pertinent people and rules of the college. This liaison will be able to advocate, coach, troubleshoot, talk to professors or the residence assistant, or do whatever is necessary to help resolve issues that crop up and make things go more smoothly for the student with Asperger Syndrome. A liaison should:

- Be someone with whom the person with Asperger Syndrome feels comfortable, so that she can turn to this person if she has any questions, feels overwhelmed or is confused by either the academic or social pressures. The liaison should be readily available for communication.
- Keep in touch with the student on a regular basis (e.g., weekly).
- Notice promptly if the student with Asperger Syndrome is experiencing stress or running into problems, and help figure out what's going on and how to improve the situation before things escalate.
- Bring to the student's attention the unwritten social rules of classroom, dorm, and campus behavior.
- Be someone who can help the student with Asperger Syndrome understand the system and make the system work for the student.
- Help the student negotiate the college bureaucracy and comply with the rules governing essentials such as registration, academic advising, meeting requirements for the chosen major area of studies and distribution requirements, graduation requirements, etc.

• Be the person to whom the student's parents can turn if they have concerns or questions about how their son or daughter is doing at school. [Note: It is not acceptable practice at most colleges for a parent to communicate concerns directly to a professor due to privacy protections for adults.]

Either on or off campus, the additional support network for a person with AS might also include any or all of the following:

a. A therapist who understands Asperger Syndrome and who can offer practical suggestions for coping with the demands of college life.

b. A social skills class to help with friendships and relationships.

c. Academic support such as tutoring in a specific subject, organizational help, or study skills.

d. A life coach or someone similar who can help the student organize different areas of his life, including financial management and staying on top of all important papers and documents.

e. A cell phone enabling contact with the student's liaison or parents in the event of difficulties and if the need for emergency assistance or guidance arises.

A support network works best if everyone who is a part of it has written permission by the student to communicate with the other members. Providing them with contact information for the other members of the support network will help them establish and maintain contact.

Start Early with Career Exploration and Planning

Earning a college degree is a wonderful accomplishment but by itself does not guarantee a job. The world is filled with unemployed and underemployed people who earned liberal arts degrees with majors such as video, photography, history, English, communications, or philosophy. A few of these people go on to graduate school and become professors but that is expensive, time-consuming, and also carries no guarantees of a job.

Consequently, it is important to set professional goals early on during the college years, and choose courses and other experiences that will help ensure that the student graduates with certain skills, concentrated knowledge, and documented experience that will give her a head start in the job market upon graduation.

Almost all colleges have a Career Services or Career Placement Office that can offer assistance in this area. Most Career Services can:

1. Provide testing, such as interest inventories, to help in identifying rewarding careers that suit a person's skills and personality.
2. Help find part-time work, volunteer opportunities, or internship experiences while a student is still in school. This real-life experience is helpful in several ways.

   (a) The student can discover what kinds of jobs – or what aspects of a job – she enjoys or hates. (Both kinds of information are useful!)

   As an undergraduate I attended an American Symphony Orchestra League orchestra management seminar in New York City. I was fascinated since the material drew from both my musical and business studies. However, I realized that I did not want to get involved with orchestral management and subsequently declined a management internship with the Springfield, Massachusetts, Symphony Orchestra. Although the field combined interesting aspects of each field, it also seemed to carry the disadvantages of both – the personality of some of the musicians and the need for conformity of the business world. Eventually, I was glad to have taken that seminar – even though it was at great expense – because I learned that orchestral management was something I did not want to do.

(b) The student can learn about the basic expectations employers have of employees – those unwritten rules that can make or break a career.

> Interning in an accounting firm would have given me the necessary experience to determine whether the type of work and culture found in this field was suitable for me. Instead I found out the hard way by taking a job with an accounting firm and getting laid off.

(c) The student gains work-related experiences to put on his resume. Besides, former supervisors can write recommendations on his behalf, giving an added advantage over other college graduates when starting the post-college job search.

(d) Employers tend to hire people they already know. Many graduates get jobs at the companies or agencies where they interned or volunteered as students.

3. Help the student find the first job after graduation. Most college Career Offices also allow their graduates to use their services to find subsequent jobs. Additionally, many schools have reciprocal agreements with other institutions, allowing students who have moved far from their college of graduation to use an office from another school closer to where they now live.

References

American Psychiatric Association. (2000). *Diagnostic and statistical manual of mental disorders of the American Psychiatric Association* (4th ed., Text Revision). Washington, DC: Author.

Attwood, A. (1998). *Asperger's syndrome.* London: Jessica Kingsley Publishers.

Autism Network International. *ANI-L principles and policies.* Available: http://www.students.uiuc.edu/~bordner/ani/ani-l-info.html.

Autism Society of America. (2002). Autism Society of America Home Page. Retrieved November 12, 2002, from www.autism-society.org.

Axline, V. (1961). *Dibs in search of self.* New York: Ballantine Books.

Bender, L. (1947). Childhood schizophrenia, clinical study of one hundred schizophrenic children. *American Journal of Orthopsychiatry, 17,* 40-56.

Bernstein, L. (1973, Oct.-Nov.). *The unanswered question.* Cambridge, MA: The Norton Lecture Series at Harvard University.

Bettelheim, B. (1967). *The empty fortress: Infantile autism and the birth of the self.* New York: Free Press.

Bundy, A., & Murray, E. (2002). Chapter 1: Sensory integration: A. Jean Ayres' theory revisited. In A. C. Bundy, E. A. Murray, & A. C. Lane (Eds.), *Sensory integration: Theory and practice* (2nd ed., pp. 1-29). Philadelphia: F. A. Davis.

Cohen, S. (2002). *Targeting autism: What we know, don't know, and can do to help young children with autism and related disorders, updated edition.* Berkeley: University of California Press.

Dolnick, E. (1998). *Madness on the couch: Blaming the victim in the heyday of psychoanalysis.* New York: Simon & Schuster.

Goffman, E. (1963). *Stigma: Notes on the management of spoiled identity.* New York: Simon and Schuster.

Grandin, T. (1995). *Thinking in pictures and other reports from my life with autism.* New York: Doubleday.

Greenspan, S., & Wieder, S. (1989). *The child with special needs: Encouraging intellectual and emotional growth.* Reading, MA: Addison-Wesley.

Johnson, C., & Crowder, J. (1994). *Autism: From tragedy to triumph.* Boston, MA: Branden Books.

Kaufman, B. (1976). *Son-rise.* New York: Harper & Row.

Kitahara, K. (1983). *A method of educating autism children: Daily life therapy: Record of actual education at Musashino Higashi Gakuen School, Japan, vol. 1, 2, & 3.* Boston, MA: Nimrod Press.

Kranowitz, C. (1998). *The out-of-sync child: Recognizing and coping with sensory integration dysfunction.* New York: Skylight Press.

Lovaas, O. I. (1987). Behavioral treatment and normal education and intellectual functioning in young autistic children. *Journal of Consulting and Clinical Psychology, 55,* 3-9.

Lovaas, O. I., & Smith, T. (1989). A comprehensive behavioral theory of autistic children: Paradigm for research and treatment. *Journal of Behavior Therapy and Experimental Psychiatry, 20,* 17-29.

Lovaas, I. (2002). *Teaching individuals with developmental delays: Basic intervention techniques.* Austin. TX: Pro-Ed Publishing Company.

Lovaas, O. I., Ackerman, A. B., Alexander, D., Firestone, P., Perkins, J., & Young, D. (1981). *Teaching developmentally disabled children: The ME book.* Austin. TX: Pro-Ed Publishing Company.

May, R. (1983). The three modes of world. In R. May, *The discovery of being: Writings in existential psychology.* New York: W.W. Norton.

McGahee, M., Mason, C., Wallace, T., & Jones, B. (2001). *Student-led IEPs: A guide for student involvement.* Arlington, VA: Council for Exceptional Children. Available at http://www.cec.sped.org/bk/catalog2/iep.html.

McGahee-Kovac, M. (2002). *A student's guide to the IEP* (2nd ed.). Washington, DC: National Information Center for Children and Youth with Disabilities. Retrieved March 23, 2002, from www.nichcy.org/pubs/stguide/st1.htm.

Miller, A. (November 19, 1999). The Miller Method website. Available: http://www.millermethod.org.

Miller, A., & Eller-Miller, E. (1973). Cognitive developmental training with elevated boards and sign language. *Journal of Autism and Childhood Schizophrenia, 3,* 65-85.

Miller, A., & Eller-Miller, E. (1989). *From ritual to repertoire: A cognitive-developmental systems approach with behavior-disordered children.* New York: Wiley-Interscience.

Myles, B. S., Cook, K., Miller, N., Rinner, L., & Robbins, L. (2000). *Asperger Syndrome and sensory issues: Practical solutions for making sense of the world.* Shawnee Mission, KS: Autism Asperger Publishing Company.

National Information Center for Children and Youth with Disabilities. (2002). *Technical assistance guide: Helping students develop their IEPs.* Washington, DC: Author. Retrieved March 23, 2002, from www.nichcy.org/pubs/stguide/ta2.htm.

Park, C. (1967). *The siege.* New York: Little & Brown.

Rank, B. (1949, January). Adaptation of the psychoanalytic technique for the treatment of children with atypical development. *American Journal of Orthopsychiatry, 19,* 130-139.

Ratey, J., & Johnson, C. (1997). *Shadow syndromes.* New York: Pantheon Books.

Ratey, J. (2001). *A user's guide to the brain: Perception, attention, and the four theaters of the brain.* New York: Pantheon Books.

Rimland, B. (1964). *Infantile autism: The syndrome and its implications for a neural theory of behavior.* New York: Appleton-Century-Crofts.

Schlaug, G., Jancke, L., Huang, Y., Stagier, J., & Steinmetz, H. (1995). Increased corpus callosum size in musicians. *Neuropsychologica, 33*(8), 1047-1055.

Schoenberg, A. (1947). *A survivor from Warsaw,* Op. 46.

Schopler, E., Reichler, R., & Lansing, M. (1980). *Teaching strategies for parents and professionals, vol. 2.* Chapel Hill: University of North Carolina.

Sellin, B. (1995). *Messages from an autistic mind: I don't want to be inside me anymore.* New York: Harper Collins.

Siegel, B. (1996). *The world of the autistic child: Understanding and treating autistic spectrum disorders.* New York: Oxford Press.

University of California Regents. (2000). *U.C. Davis M.I.N.D. Institute Receives $30 Million in State Funding.* Retrieved November 11, 2002, from http://news.ucdmc.ucdavis.edu/MIND_StateFunding.html.

Willey, L. (1999). *Pretending to be normal: Living with Asperger's Syndrome.* Philadelphia, PA: Jessica Kingsley.

Williams, D. (1992). *Nobody nowhere: The extraordinary autobiography of an autistic.* New York: Times Books.

Wobus, J. (2000, May 12). *Autism resources.* Available: http://www.autismresources.com/autism/nonfictionyears/index.html.

CPSIA information can be obtained
at www.ICGtesting.com
Printed in the USA
LVHW012321270821
696293LV00002B/294

9 781931 282192

Thanks for being a part of Slingshot. Here's some helpful information on how to use the Slingshot service to its fullest.

Everyone wants you to have the best experience possible. While we're available during convenient business hours, your Slingshot account is available 24/7/365.

From your Slingshot account, you can:

- Manage your account and preferences
- See when your rentals are due, or purchase more time
- Access your digital course materials
- Look up price and condition information for your books

To access your Slingshot account:

1. Go to **slingshotedu.com**
2. Click the **LOGIN** button on the top right corner
3. Select your school
4. You already have an account – follow the prompts to enter your login credentials

slingshotedu.com

General FAQ's

What if I need to return a book?
Contact Customer Support, or bring it to the closest campus store for assistance. You can return any book for any reason up to seven days after your class begins, with no restocking fees.

I just added a class. How do I get my books?
When a class is added, an order will automatically be created for you. You'll receive an email when the materials you need have been shipped to you, or are ready to be picked up on campus.

What if an item is missing from my order?
Check if the book is listed on the "**Items not in this shipment**" section of your packing list. If it is, this item will either be digital or coming in a separate box. You will receive emails from us about the additional item(s). If you are missing a book in any other circumstance, contact us for assistance as soon as possible.

My book is a little banged up. Will I be responsible for the damage?
If you're concerned with the condition of your textbook, contact us within a week of receiving it. We'll help you find a solution.

What do I do with my rental books at the end of class?
Physical rental textbooks are due back at the end of class. These are indicated by the word **Rental** on your packing slip, under which you will find the due date for that book. When you're ready to return your rentals, bring them to the designated location on campus or return them by mail through your Slingshot account. Rental due dates will also be found under the **"My Course Materials"** tab. Digital rental books expire automatically.

What if I decide to keep a rental book, or I miss the rental due date?
You can keep a rental and we'll bill the rental not returned (RNR) fee to your Student account. The buyout fee is the purchase price of the book less the amount you already paid for the rental. If you miss the rental due dates, RNRs can be refunded for 14 days after they are billed, minus a restocking fee.

Will I always get my textbook type preference (i.e. rent, buy used, buy new)?
Most of the time, but not always. We start by trying to fill your requirements according to the preference you select. However, sometimes there may not be a used copy of a book available, and certain types of books cannot be rented — workbooks or textbooks with access codes, for example.